MW01595231

Did Your Grandfather Steal My Christmas Present?

American and German Stories of the Second World War

Did Your Grandfather Steal My Christmas Present?
Copyright © 2003 by Betsy Richardson Pingen

All rights reserved.
Printed and bound in America. Except as permitted under the United States
Copyright Act of 1976, no part of this may be reproduced or distributed in
any form or stored in a data base or retreival system without prior written
permission from the publisher or author.

Library of Congress number pending --
First Edition First Printing December 2003
ISBN # 0-9748591-4-1

Published by Main Street Publishing Inc., Jackson,Tn. Printed and bound by
NetPub Corp., Poughkeepsie, New York. Written by
Betsy Richardson Pingen. Cover idea by Betsy Richardson Pingen. Editing
by Michael F. Duke and Annette Galloway.

For information on this publication write: Main Street Publishing Inc.206
East Main Street, Suite 207 P.O. Box 696, Jackson, Tn. 38302E-
Mail:words@mspbooks.comWebsites: www.mspbooks.com and
www:mainstreetpublishing.com.
Phone: 731-427-7379   1-866-457-7379

Did Your Grandfather Steal My Christmas Present?

American and German Stories of the Second World War

By Betsy Pingen

Main Street Publishing, Inc.   Jackson, Tn.

Preface

We had been dating three weeks when I brought Georg Pingen home to meet all of my relatives. We were seniors in high school, and Georg was my first boyfriend. He had come to the United States for one year as a foreign exchange student from Germany. I loved listening to his accent and questioned him extensively regarding the differences between the United States and Germany, but it was not until I introduced him to my grandfather that I truly grasped the significance of his nationality.

It was my grandmother's birthday, and Georg and I arrived late. Every grandparent, aunt, uncle, and cousin was there, and I led my first boyfriend from one relative to another, proudly but nervously introducing him. Everyone seemed to like him, and he seemed to feel comfortable with all of them. It was an atmosphere of celebration and laughter-until I came to the last introduction. I led Georg into the dining room where my grandfather, whom I call Popo, was finishing a piece of birthday cake. I introduced my new boyfriend by name and nationality, as I had done with everyone else. However, upon hearing that Georg was from Germany, my grandfather did not extend his hand or respond with a word of greeting. Instead, he asked quietly but bluntly, "Did your grandfather steal my Christmas present?"

I swallowed hard. What kind of question was that? I looked to Georg and saw him standing there dumbfounded.

He seemed to struggle to find a response but could not. I looked around the room and saw that we were not alone. Everyone in the room had stopped their conversations and had turned toward my grandfather with confused stares. After a few uncomfortable moments, Popo continued, "When I was in France, some German soldiers stole our Christmas packages, and I never did find out what my mother sent me." His smile eased everyone's fears, signifying he was only joking. Conversation and laughter filled the room once more. However, it was with that encounter that I realized that our grandfathers had been enemies in the most deadly war ever fought. How then was it possible for us, their grandchildren, only two generations later, to be the best of friends-and ultimately husband and wife?

Introduction

From the night of Popo's startling question, I knew that I wanted to, or perhaps even needed to, know more about the peculiar relationship between our grandfathers. However, I knew that would be a daunting undertaking. My grandfather's comment to Georg was the first time I had ever heard him speak of the war. There was a longstanding, unspoken rule in our family that Popo did not talk about the war and no one was supposed to ask. However, even if I broke this accepted code of silence, I still had to find out what happened to Georg's grandfathers. And if I could not talk about the war with my own family, how could I ask people whom, at the time, I barely knew? I needed an excuse.

Two years later an assignment in a college German course presented me with that excuse. I was supposed to write a three-page paper and make a short presentation on any topic of interest to me related to German culture. After some deliberation, I decided that I would attempt to compare an American "Soldier" and a German "Soldat." Maybe, if I told them it was for a school assignment, Popo and Georg's family would tell me about the war.

Sure enough, on Thanksgiving Day I sat down to talk with my grandfather about his experiences during the Second World War. Popo began, "We shipped out on Thanksgiving Day." With that simple sentence, a knot formed in his throat, and tears began flowing down his face. He put his face in his hands;

he could not continue. It was at that instant that I realized this was much more than a class project. I would not be able to turn it in and forget about it. With the first tear that rolled down Popo's face, I learned more about World War II than I had ever learned in any history book. What happened more than fifty years ago that still causes an old man to cry?

However, that was not the end of my research and interviews. I soon turned my interest to the other side of the world, to Germany. I was uncertain and scared of what I might find there. Was it even acceptable to ask about the war? After all, my grandfather had rarely ever spoken about it and had broken down into tears when I had asked, and he was one of the "heroes," "the good guys." What would be the reaction of those who had been on the other side of the line, "the enemies?"

I first asked Georg's grandmother if I might interview her about her experiences some time. She immediately began telling me stories. She later commented, "You're the only one who's ever cared about this stuff. My grandchildren would all just say, 'Oh, stop it, Grandma. That's enough of your old stories.'" The other Germans I interviewed all responded similarly; they could talk for hours without my asking any questions. I slowly realized that this was a generation who had so much to tell but feared that no one wanted to listen.

As I have already mentioned, I first began this project for a college German class at Samford University. We were assigned to make a ten-minute oral presentation about some aspect of German culture. After I had compiled the stories of my grandfather, the "Soldier", and Georg's grandfather, the "Soldat," I tried to practice the presentation in front of Georg. After one hour of a tongue-tied struggle, I was frustrated and discouraged. I stopped and looked at my one-man audience; he was growing bored and impatient. I lay down on the bed and cried. I enjoy public speaking and can usually do so effectively; why then was this so difficult? Georg asked me why I was so upset; he tried to tell me that with a little work, it would be fine. As we talked to one another, I began to understand the reason I was doing this and why it meant so much to me. I was not doing the project for myself, but rather for Popo. I wanted this to somehow be a tribute for all that he had done and for all that he had suffered. It was for Georg's grandfathers, for our families and for all the soldiers that had fought in that war. For that reason, I wanted this to be perfect, but nothing I could say in a ten-minute presentation, or for that matter in a year-long presentation, could say what Popo had said sitting on the couch with tears rolling down his face.

Somehow I did make it through that first speech (although not in ten minutes), and at that point, I realized that the project had only begun. I expanded my research to include all four of our grandfathers. After talking to the wives about their husbands' experiences, I found the grandmothers' war stories to be equally as compelling, and I decided to include their experiences as well. One year after I had begun the project, I completed my senior thesis, Soldier and Soldat: The Tears and Silence of the Second World War.

The largest part of my research was spent listening. I recorded and transcribed each interview because I knew that I could never retell the stories the way our grandparents had told them. They were their stories and their lives. They could only be told in their words. In my research I also had the opportunity to explore the contents of many dusty old shoeboxes, treasure chests used on both sides of the Atlantic to preserve the black and white photographs, the worn, yellowed letters, and the odds and ends that tell the stories of so many lives.

This book is divided into two parts: Grandfathers and Grandmothers. For each individual I had different sources of information available to me. I was able to personally interview most of the people in the book and was able to hear their stories firsthand. I was able to ask them questions to find out details and was limited only by their memories and emotions. Unfortunately, both of Georg's grandfathers had already passed away when I began my research. Although I could not interview them personally, I was able to learn of their experiences through diaries, letters, and interviews with their friends and relatives.

This book is not intended to be a history book, although it contains history. The stories that make up this book are not historical facts but rather are the remnants of occurrences and emotions that have lain dormant in human minds for more than half a century. The people in this book are telling their stories after fifty years of silence, and as Popo said, "Fifty years wipes away a lot of memories." Although many people from the World War II generation faced similar circumstances and shared similar feelings with those described in this book, the book itself is not designed to be representative of the experiences of veterans or of those on the home front. It is simply a book about two families, one German and one American, separated by an ocean and a war, later united by their grandchildren.

Part I

Our Grandfathers

Doyle Porter Richardson
Born: July 12, 1924

**42nd Infantry Rainbow Division
242nd Infantry Regiment
Company C**

Chapter 1

Popo: A Soldier's Tears

"I have to ask him. I have to ask him," I repeated to myself over and over as my parents, my brother, my boyfriend, and I drove to my grandparents' house on Thanksgiving Day, 1999. I was trying to gather the courage to shatter a long-respected family silence; I wanted to ask my grandfather Popo about the Second World War. When I had formed the idea for my research project, it had sounded simple enough. I would compare the war experiences of my grandfather with the experiences of my German boyfriend's (now husband's) grandfather. All I had to do was ask my grandfather what he had done during the war. Then I would ask my boyfriend's grandmother what her husband had done (because his grandfather had already passed away). Then I would only need to record what they told me. I would be finished, and the project should be interesting.

Then I began to contemplate the technicalities of the project. I would have to ask Popo about the war. I began to think about what I already knew and realized that I had never heard my grandfather talk about the war. I had never heard anyone ask him about it. He, along with my grandmother, aunt, and uncle, had gone to Germany in 1995 for the fiftieth anniversary of the end of World War II. When they came back, they had talked about the trip, about the food, the weather, the landscape, and the people they had met. However, they never mentioned the war itself or the memories that must have been evoked by the journey.

I vaguely remembered having seen a map with the route of Popo's division outlined on it, and I remembered that one point had been marked with the words "Lost most of our battalion here." From that, I knew that the war must have been a nightmarish experience for him. I tried to imagine him in many of the war scenes that I had seen in movies. I tried to imagine him with a young face full of intensity covered with the dirt and grime of war wearing a soldier's helmet while bombs exploded around him. I could not. I could only see his wrinkled face with a quiet smile and twinkling eyes as he watched his baby great-granddaughter play.

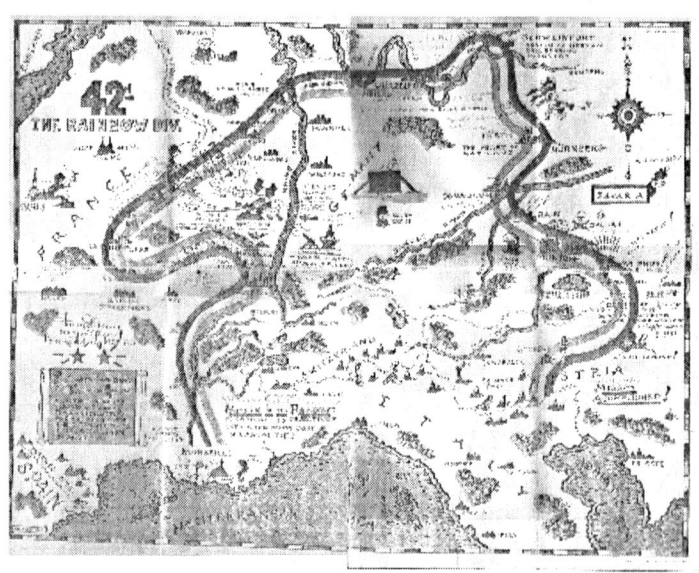

(above) Map of the route of the Rainbow Division

(above) Popo with son Gary Richardson, Grandson Ryan Richardson, and great-grandaughter Page Richardson.

I had heard about veterans who could not talk about their war experiences. If they tried, they cried and trembled. They had nightmares and flashbacks. They became violently angry. What would Popo do?

My grandfather was 75 years old when I interviewed him. His life is typical of a man who grew up and lived in the rural South. He is retired and lives with his wife in Gadsden, Tennessee, a small town with a population of about 500. He has lived there all of his life, and the house he now calls home is right next door to the house in which he grew up. Before he retired, he had owned a Texaco station and a small farm. He has three children, my father among them, four grandchildren, and one great-granddaughter, all of whom live within a few miles of his home. He is famous for his garden, where he grows everything from watermelons to squash, and for his dry sense of humor. His one-line jokes seem to come from nowhere, and he is the only one who can tell them without the hint of a smile.

Popo is generally a very pleasant and approachable man, and therefore, I was surprised to find myself sitting in the car that Thanksgiving Day afraid to talk to him. But a cloud of silence surrounded his experiences in World War II. I was stepping into the unknown, and I could not know what I might find. Nonetheless, in order to make my report, I would have to shatter that silence; there was no other way. Would Popo be angry with me for asking? Would he cry? Would he just refuse to talk about it?

Before we had left our house, I had asked my father if he thought it would be okay to ask Popo about the war. He thought about it for a moment and then nodded. My mother objected, "Are you sure?" My dad answered, "If we're ever going to know about it, he has to tell us now." Needless to say, that response did nothing to calm my fears.

At my grandparents' house, we filled ourselves with turkey and dressing and all of the traditional Thanksgiving dishes. However, most of my food seemed to stay in my throat as I pondered how I could bring up the dreaded topic. After everyone was uncomfortably full, we all went into the living room and sat down in the chairs and on the floor. I sat next to Popo on the couch. Everyone was laughing and exchanging stories, but then all of the conversations seemed to cease. My boyfriend, Georg, interrupted the silence to ask my uncle (who was in the military) if he could interview him about the Cold War. (He was also working on a paper for a history class.) I knew this was the time to ask my grandfather, so I turned and quickly and timidly asked, "Popo, after they are finished, could I interview you about World War II?" I am sure that I said it so quickly that it all sounded as one word, but he understood and slowly nodded his head.

Georg began talking to my uncle, but I was barely listening.

My muscles were tense, and my heart was pounding. "Now what?" I wondered. "Do I ask specific questions or just ask him to talk?" The interview about the Cold War seemed very short, too short. It had gone very smoothly; now, if only mine would be so easy.

I decided just to let my grandfather talk. After all, it would be more meaningful if he told me what he thought was important, and maybe that would help avoid any uncomfortable topics. He was not quite sure where to begin, so I asked him, "Were you drafted? How old were you?" With his deep, grunted voice and slow Southern drawl, he answered, "I was 19 when they drug me in." And with that his story began to unfold.

Popo had just graduated from high school and was helping his father on their 200-acre farm in Gadsden when he was drafted. He lived in a three-room house with his parents, an older sister (Martha), and a younger brother (Pomvelle). He was at home when he got the notice telling him to report to Alamo, Tennessee, on April 7, 1944. He was expecting the notice, for he had already been called in for a physical examination. At the physical, men were assigned to various classifications, 1-A and 4-F being the most common. Popo was classified as 1-A, the most likely to be drafted. Thirteen men from the county were ordered to report to Alamo that day.

My grandfather was sent to the Induction Center in Camp Shelby, Mississippi. Three days later he was sent to Camp Wheeler in Macon, Georgia. "That was the furthest from home I'd ever been." There he spent 17 weeks being trained as a Communications Officer.

When I had begun the interview, my grandmother had gone to one of the rooms in the back of the house and had returned with a shoebox. The box was filled with crinkled, yellowed documents and black-and-white photographs. Popo picked up one of the photos, a picture of his unit at Camp Wheeler. He pointed to one of the young men, and said:

I can't think of his name, but he was a Polock from New Jersey. He was small, thin, and we was taking our last march down there [at Camp Wheeler], and they said if we didn't make it, we'd have to take it over. And he give out just about as far from here to Gadsden, so I took his field bag and carried it with mine. And he made it. After that, he just really took up to me. And he had a friend from New Jersey that he graduated with; he sent her my name and address, and she started writing me and sending me pictures, and she was a beautiful thing, prettier than my girlfriend back home. I don't know what become of that picture. It was lying on my dresser upstairs at Mama's all these years. She was pretty; she wanted to come to Tennessee when I come home on leave; that's the last I heard from her. I had to stop that. My girlfriend back home fell in love with somebody else while I was gone, evidently. She waited; she was still here, and I went with her several times after I got back, but then she married somebody else.

Popo, high school graduation, 1943

(below) At Camp Wheeler, Georgia. Popo is on the
second row, far right.

Popo was sent home for nine days in July "on a train that stopped at every house on the way." He then traveled to Corinth, Mississippi and from there to Fort Meade, Maryland. "There, they told me, 'We don't need no communications; we need riflemen.'" And so Popo was retrained as a rifleman. He was then sent to Camp Gruber, Oklahoma.

We weren't all rejects, but many was, up at Camp Gruber. If they was kicked out of any other branch, they put 'em in the infantry. We had one boy from the Naval Academy that was supposed to get his wings to fly the next day, and he got drunk the night before, they kicked him out, and he came to Camp Gruber. You talk about a sick boy. He disobeyed every order that was given and was always on KP. We got over there, overseas, got on the front lines. He was ordered to dig a latrine for the officers. He said, "If they gotta take a crap, they can dig their own damn hole." Of course, he did that purposely, and they court marshaled him. He stayed in prison all the time we was over there. I think Captain Duffy helped get him out after the war. He was from a real affluent family evidently, had lots of money. Every ten minute break we took while we was in training down there, he kept a diary, so I imagine he had some experiences while he was in prison because they said they were tough on them, anybody that got court marshaled. They didn't have any contact with home either.

One boy at Camp Gruber says, "What are the division's colors- red, yellow, and blue." He said, "We'll never see any blood, we're yellow, and we'll never see any damn water." He was very wrong. It wasn't another day, and they shipped us out.

Popo stayed in Oklahoma until November, where they "trained and trained and trained with those rifles." One night he received a call telling him to put all troops on alert. Popo was on guard duty and had to relay the message. Two or three days later they loaded up and took a train to Camp Kilmer, New Jersey.

"We boarded the ship on Thanksgiving Day, 1944." The words stuck in his throat, and tears began flowing down his cheeks. His eyes glazed over, and I knew he was seeing images and reliving experiences that no one else could see or understand. He covered his face with his hands and tried to apologize between the sobs, saying that he had not realized it had been 55 years ago to the day. Everyone in the room stared at the floor, at the ceiling, anywhere but at my grandfather's face. No one knew what to say, and after several minutes of this uncomfortable silence, interrupted only by Popo's sobs, one of my relatives began talking about a neighbor's health problems. It was an attempt to change the subject, and it worked. Soon everyone began talking and laughing again. Relieved, I closed my notebook and lay it aside.

"We landed in Marseilles, France, on December 7." Everyone turned to hear the voice filled with controlled emotion. Popo was going to continue his story. I reopened my notebook and began recording.

They crossed the Atlantic on a ship called the General George M. Black. The journey took them about two weeks. Once they arrived in France, they loaded onto trucks about ten miles outside of Marseilles.

It was colder than here. We stayed in 2-man tents and were told that we would take a bath and shave each day, but we didn't take off our clothes because it was so cold. This one little boy was climbing on the side of the truck. We was fixing to go out to our area, and all he could say was "Gum chum." Of course, he'd take anything we'd give him. He was going from one to another, "Gum chum, gum chum." They were in pitiful shape.

They took the trucks to a railway where they boarded the forty-and-eight rail cars that were left over from World War I. (They were called forty-and-eights because they could hold forty mules and eight men.) They traveled for several days on the train at about three miles per hour. Thankfully there had been enough people in the car to keep it warm.

They stopped somewhere in southern France. From there they moved two or three times before they finally found themselves in Hatten, France. They were at Hatten when they encountered the Battle of the Bulge. "It was right before Christmas." I heard the emotion rising in my grandfather's voice. "It had snowed and snowed and snowed." He began to cry but determined to fight through the tears. "Somebody got sick, and I had to go take their guard duty on the other side of the town. That saved my life." He paused. "It was a 2 1/2 hour shift, but after 1 1/2 hours, all hell broke loose." With the last sentence, he covered his face with his hands, and through his tears murmured, "Had it easy compared to what some did."

He was not able to say anymore that day about the battle at Hatten, but a few weeks later, he did continue the story:

It was about Christmas time, we'd just got our mail one day. It was late; it came in during the night. Our jeeps were parked in a barn or some kind of shed there, and it was full of Christmas packages. That's how come me to ask Georg if his grandfather stole my Christmas package. They hit us just before daylight early one morning. They sent me out at 3:00 to the outer part of town as a guard, security guard, me and another boy. Of course there was others, too, but me and him were together, and we were the further ones out. The Germans hit from the opposite direction, and we didn't know what was going on for, oh, eight hours, I guess. I mean, we saw what was going on, but we didn't see any personnel. We was dodging bullets, but we didn't know where they was coming from or who was shooting them.

Popo at the Hatten/Rittershoffen Monument that testifies
to the battle faught there.

Popo revisiting Hatten, France in 1995

He further explained:

The 222nd, 232nd, and 242nd regiments were all a battalion. I don't know how many battalions it takes to make a division, but it was about 18,000 of us that left Camp Gruber. When we got over there and got hit, our division headquarters was still in Gruber, so we weren't even counted as being over there. The headquarters is the main part of it, regardless where the rest of us are. We were over there without a country, you might say. We were over there; we didn't have any artillery or anything to shoot back at those German tanks. We just had our little rifles, maybe some mortar. I think there was some mortar, but we weren't set up for that on a surprise attack.

"And that was where your Christmas packages disappeared?" my grandmother interrupted. My grandfather continued:

Yeah. They got our jeeps and everything. We captured one of our jeeps back before the war was over. The reason we knew it is because Wiggins from Kansas was the jeep driver. He'd had a wreck sometime after he'd started driving that jeep, and one of his teeth were buried up in the steering wheel of that jeep. It was still in there when we got it back. [My army buddy] Hank hears from Wiggins every once in a while. He was a character. He was the company driver.

During the Thanksgiving Day interview, Popo paused and took a moment to collect his emotions after attempting to talk about the battle at Hatten. He then continued his story. He was stationed with one other soldier on the other side of the town. When their shift was over, no one came to replace them. They did not leave their post. After a full day had passed, however, Popo decided that they should leave, but the other soldier refused. Finally, Popo left by himself. He hid in the loft of a barn and ate apples that had been stored there. After several days he recognized American voices underneath him and climbed down to join them. They could see out of the windows that the Germans were going through all of the neighboring buildings with tanks, and they knew they had to make a run for it.

He described the situation as if he were still seeing it, "I seen, when I was getting out of Hatten, we had to step over bodies." He began to cry uncontrollably, and his whole body shook with emotion. "It was Germans and Americans." He could not continue, and my grandmother tried to fill in the uncomfortable silence, "I don't think anybody knows what all of them have been through, and so many people don't care anymore. We take all this for granted until you pursue and find out what really went on. We don't give recognition where it's due. In our area, you were talking about who went: Edward Williams and Porter, who else in Gadsden?"

"Floyd," Popo answered with controlled emotion.

"Floyd Rea, Mrs. Jean's husband, but there was a lot of people in the military that were not actually, you know, involved."

My grandfather interjected, "They say it took seven to have one man on the front line."

"They were supporting but not actually doing the..." As she was in the middle of her sentence, my grandfather interrupted her, as though she were not talking and as though there had been no interruption in his story:

I don't know whether they was all killed there or not; they might of froze to death. They couldn't even pick up these soldiers for days, and finally the Germans ran out of fuel. They couldn't operate for a time, and we did, too. They were all at a standstill there. They sent in all these big trucks and picked up these bodies, just lines of trucks full of bodies.

The tears began to well up in his eyes once again. "Where was this?" my grandmother asked. "Hatten. Battle of the Bulge, they called it."

Popo, along with the other American soldiers, managed to escape from the barn. "Our tanks, Patton's tanks came in five or seven days later because they'd found out some of us were still in there." After he had rejoined the American troops, he learned that only 17 from his company of 180 had survived the battle.

I saw the gleam return to my grandfather's eye, and a tight smile came across his lips. "I had 41 cents in my pocket when I got on that ship," he said.

One of my relatives asked the obvious question, "How did you get down to 41 cents? Playing poker?"

My grandfather shook his head.

Shooting dice. The sergeant in my platoon had a pair of dice that probably wasn't anything but sixes on them. And he was doing all the rolling, and I never did see those dice. A hundred and something dollars, I done forgot what it was that I lost.

"It's about like going to Tunica, isn't it?" someone added, referring to Popo's recent trips to Tunica, Mississippi, known for its casinos.

Faster than that. I never did see those dice, but I know he couldn't keep rolling all those twelve's every time. I stuck that 41 cents in my pocket, and I still had it when I got back home. I reckon it's still in there somewhere. It mighta' got mixed up in the shuffle, I don't know.

Popo looked at me. "See, you can make it over there with less," he said, referring to my several trips to Europe on which I had obviously spent much more than 41 cents.

"Sergeant Price let me borrow forty dollars when we was over there. I was gonna pay him back when we got home." My grandfather looked down at his hands. "I guess I still owe him that forty dollars. He didn't make it back."

After Hatten, it took a week to get them all back shuffled in. Popo was promoted to sergeant and was put in charge of some of the new recruits. It was then that Hank and Casey, war buddies with whom my grandfather is still friends, joined his company. At the 1995 reunion of Company C in Jekyll Island, Georgia, Popo asked one of the other men if he could remember Casey. The man answered, "Yeah, the contrariest bastard in our company, the bitchinest, complainenest..."

My grandmother explained, "He was just a spoiled brat, and the minute he got 18, they drafted him. He'd just finished high school, and he said he still had his security blanket, and he said Porter took his security blanket."

"And his teddy bear and his bottle," Popo added with a gentle grunt of laughter.

Mema continued, "After he was telling about Porter taking all that away from him, we bought a baby blanket and a baby bottle and a teddy bear and mailed it to him for Christmas. He accused Porter of taking all that away, so we sent him a package for Christmas." Popo decided to add his own stories about Casey:

Our field jacket had a hood you could pull over your head, kind of keep your ears warm. This was after Hatten, when he first joined us. We had to go on field trials to acclimatize the new recruits to the darkness and all. They all thought we were old veterans who'd been over there at least a year, and we'd only been there two more weeks than they had. So I was taking my recruits out one night to do a little patrolling, and Casey pulled that hood up over his head and stood there. Zero degree weather, stomping in the snow. I didn't know him very well, and he didn't know me either; none of us knew each other. We'd never been together before, so I jerked that headliner off and said, "Boy, if you can't hear what's going on, somebody'll shoot your damn head off." And he said, "Hell, I'd rather be shot than froze to death."

(From left to right) Popo, Eugene Casey, and another soldier from Company C.

Eugene Casey and Popo at their first reunion since
the war in Germany, 1995.

Casey's mother used to send the best packages. He said sometimes
we'd wait until he got off duty before we'd open them. He shared.
But she'd send a great big ol' box. Ain't no telling how much she
was out for postage, sending all that stuff over there. He was a
Catholic and about thirty days before Lent, they leave off the food,
and he had all that food stored up. You'd think it was a small grocery
store when that day was over. Aw, he lit into that, and he was sick
for a month.

My grandmother added, "And they would all go out and
get drunk on Saturday night, and then they'd go to the priest
to confess. He got all these guys that were Catholics to go
with him, not Porter, but some of the other guys."

"Fifteen or twenty of 'em," my grandfather chimed in
and began telling the story.

The sister, the nun, came to the door and Casey was talking about that they was gonna confess. His mother had sent him a little card with what to confess for in their language [French or German], and he was showing the nun that. Then she said, "Oh, Father So-and-So can speak perfect English." Casey said he looked behind his head, and every one of them other boys had disappeared. He was left standing by himself. They didn't want nobody to understand what they'd been doing.

The corners of Popo's eyes wrinkled with laughter as he finished the story. "You really have to hear him tell that. Casey has some tales."

After the companies had been regrouped following Hatten, they went back in to battle on March 3, 1945. "Us Americans was on one side of the Rhine River, and Germans was on the other, but it was so cold that neither of us could do nothing." Popo did not say much more about what he encountered during the next two months before the war ended.

We went through Germany pretty fast, you see. There was a big sign up there as we entered: "Do not fraternize with the Germans." I wonder if that sign's still there. It was right at the top. What's that line called up through there? The Siegfried Line. That's where the sign was. We had just about as much propaganda shot to us as they did. We had dummies out in our area in basic training. We was actually fighting a dummy, but it was a German or a Jap one. We was pretty well filled with hatred at the time.

My grandfather continued his explanation about his feelings for the Germans by telling a story from his visit to Germany in 1995.

POCKET GUIDE TO

This booklet is issued in the interest of informing you about the country you occupy. Nothing contained herein should be considered a relaxation of the Non-Fraternization Policy.

Keep faith with the American soldiers who have died to eliminate the German warmakers.

DO NOT FRATERNIZE

Germany

The cover of the booklet American soldiers recieved
before entering Germany.

Popo with Henry Wilkins

Soldiers from Popo's company

We were in the Dachau area when this mayor talked to us. He said he was going to be ten years old the day after we took that town. He had had his uniform laying out on the bed that he was to wear. It's like when our boys would be Boy Scouts. I don't know what they would be, but it was building them up to serve in the army. He already had the uniform, but he couldn't use it until the next day. He said he hated us Americans because he didn't get to wear his new suit. We took the town on the ninth, and he was supposed to get to wear it on the tenth, when he'd be ten years old.

I think that was the beginning of me feeling different about the Germans because I always thought of them as Hitler. The dummies that we fought in basic training all had Hitler on them. It wasn't Germans; it was Hitler. So I thought of all Germans as Hitler. That's all we heard about. We didn't hear nothing about German people that had any feelings or families. Of course, they gotta put that to you to get you to fight. They gotta do it to young people to get them to fight.

I read other sources about Popo's division and learned that the division began its attack at Wingen, France. They pushed through the Hardt Mountains and the Siegfried Line past Dahn, Germany. In April they captured Würzburg, Schweinfurt, Furth, and Donauworth.

On April 29, 1945, they liberated the concentration camp in Dachau, Germany. My grandfather did not mention the liberation when he talked about the war. When he visited Germany in 1995, they held a memorial service at the concentration camp to honor those who had helped to liberate it and to remember those who had suffered and died there. Popo waited outside. He could not and did not go back there. Some horrors are indeed too terrible to be remembered.

The division swept through Munich on April 30 shortly before the war ended on May 8. Popo recounted his recollections of the ending of the war:

They set a date three or four days before the war was over for it to be over. It just couldn't be over. It had to fall on a certain date. I don't know why they couldn't have stopped when they decided to stop. The day that the war was over, the fields and roads were just full of German soldiers surrendering to us rather than the Russians. We were just over the hill from the Russians, and the Germans didn't want to be captured by them. The roads and fields wouldn't hold them all. They was on bicycles, motorcycles, horses, and walking.

May 8, 1945 may have marked the official end of the war, but it was not the end for most of the soldiers, and Popo was no exception. The soldiers received points to determine who would be sent home first. The points were based on whether the soldiers were married or had kids, how long they had been in the war, and other such factors. "I don't know how many points you needed to get to come home, but I know I had about three at the end of the war, and that wasn't near enough." Popo was sent to help guard a prisoner-of-war camp in Hallein, Austria.

We had 7,000 prisoners in that camp in Hallein. Not all of them were German prisoners because the Germans had recruited soldiers from everywhere that they had occupied. Some of them were Russians. I remember there was one big, red-headed Russian fellow, stood out there in the courtyard day after day, just looking toward the east. Won't say anything to nobody, just standing there. Great big fella'. Some of them would try to get out, crawl under the fence.

My grandmother broke in, "Some of them probably did get out, didn't they?" A grim expression fell over Popo's face, and he answered quietly, "They didn't get very far if they did. Our orders were to shoot." He continued talking about his memories of the prison.

The prison that we stayed in after the war, or that we guarded, wasn't necessarily a prison, as such, but they were enclosed. There was a hospital in there with wounded Germans, and I don't know what all nationalities were in there. They was checking them out, releasing some, and I don't know what all they was going to do with the others. I think the 101st Airborne occupied the prison before we took over, and when they walked into the hospital room, that patient had to stand up and stand at attention. If they just had one leg, they still had to prop up. It was rough on them. Our troops were mean, too, some of them. But we were taught to be mean, just like Georg's granddaddies were taught. Of course, we was all young and didn't care either.

They took a hundred prisoners up into the Alps each morning, and they cut wood all day long. The next day that hundred would stay down and sharpen saws and cook while another group went up. They were in charge of furnishing enough wood for Salzburg and one other town (the name of which Popo could not remember). They stacked the logs as high as they could on a trail. As he described how the trail wound around the mountain and how they brought the logs down, Popo once again choked on his words and began to cry. With his forehead in his hand, he said in a whisper, "It was dangerous work, but we didn't lose a man." Everyone in the room exchanged confused looks with one another. Why was he crying? Before, we had been able to form some idea as to why he was crying. He had been describing combat and death, but now the war was over, and he had just said that they "didn't lose a man." We could only imagine the atrocities that must have circulated in his mind.

As if the memory had just popped into his head, Popo said, "Those prisoners ate my dog." When everyone stared at him, he continued, "Meat was scarce over there."

My grandmother said, "Casey said you could kill a cow if it was charging you. They killed somebody's cow, didn't they?" Popo took up the story:

A woman and a girl was leading that cow to the house when those soldiers killed it, slaughtered it, and cooked it-American soldiers. It was the only cow that woman had. Casey just knew about that; he wasn't the one to kill it.

Popo then began describing the Austrian family with whom he had lived in Hallein while he guarded the POW's.

I lived with a family for almost all the time I was there after the war. I lived upstairs. They had two or three little boys and a girl. The girl was about 13 or 14. Those little boys were six, seven, eight, something like that. There was a man living there, and I never did know the connection. I don't know whether he was a brother to this woman, or they were living together or what because I couldn't understand them and they couldn't understand me. They invited me to have Christmas dinner with them. They set me a plate at the table with all this food, and they just sat around and watched me. They didn't sit down and eat, and of course I couldn't eat. We'd been eating all day. We'd had a big lunch down at our mess hall, but I tried my best to eat. It was the best they had, but it was different from ours. I didn't know what it was, and they had this steaming cup of-I thought it was probably tea. I gulped down a big swallow of that, and it was cognac. But they were real nice.

Every time I'd get a package from home, after the war while I was living with these Austrians, those little kids would come up and hold out their hands, and I'd give them something. That's what they came up for, but they was up there all day anyway. Their mother would get hot at them.

I couldn't find that particular house when we was over there in '95; it's all been torn down. Of course, it's a new project there altogether. I couldn't even find where the prison was. Of course, I wasn't expecting there to be a fence still there, or the barracks that they had lived in, but fifty years wipes away a lot of memories, and no body even remembered it.

Popo finally got the orders that allowed him to go home. He left Austria and went to Bremerhafen, Germany. There he met a friend that he knew from his hometown, which was quite impressive considering the small size of Gadsden.

Popo with his dog in Austria

Popo with his dog in Austria

Popo revisits Hallein, Austria, where he guarded
prisoners in a POW camp, picture taken in 1995

Charles Lloyd spotted me in the ice cream line; I bet that line was as long as from here to Buddy and Jan's [300 yards]-just for one little cone of ice cream. Charles Lloyd's jaws were wired together; he couldn't hardly talk. Some boy beat the stuffing out of him. He couldn't eat nothing but soup, except ice cream.

From that port Popo boarded the Blue Ridge Victory for a "nine day cruise in a three-day storm." Fortunately, he never became sick, but there were many who did. No one was excused from guard duty. "They told me to drag them up there anyway."

They landed in Camp Kilmer, New Jersey and then took a train to Camp Atterbury, Indiana. Popo was honorably discharged on June 17, 1946, and he returned home to Gadsden, Tennessee. His regiment received the Presidential Citation for their bravery and performance at Hatten.

After Popo had finished telling his story, we sorted through the old shoebox that my grandmother had found. Inside were old photographs, my grandfather's soldier hat, ration stamps, and letters. We read each of the letters in the order they had been written and followed Popo through the war. We could not help but laughing, as it became more and more obvious that my grandfather was a farmer first and a soldier second. Following are three of these letters.

Somewhere in Germany
May 6, 1945

Dear Mom, Dad, & Pomvelle,

I will try and answer your letters that I received a few days ago, sure was glad to hear from you. Pomvelle, I'm sure glad you got rid of the mumps so you could go back to school. I've been in the infirmary for the past two days to get rid of a cold and a cough, it wasn't bad but didn't seem like I could get rid of it any other way. While I'm here, I will get my teeth fixed. One of the fillings have fallen out. After I get them fixed, guess I'll return to duty because my cold has cleared up.

I received a letter from Denton [Popo's brother-in-law] the day that I received yours, said that he thought he would be there until June. I sure hope he can stay that long if not longer. Said he had a real good time while at home. The war news sure sounds good for the past few days if its only true, guess you know more about it than I do. I must close for this time and write another letter while waiting for the dentist. I'm really going to enjoy it, I know. Tell all hello.

All my love, Porter

Popo in Austria

Popo met neighbor Charles Lloyd
in Bremerhausen, Germany

Mema and Popo in 2000

Somewhere in Germany
May 8, 1945

Dear Mom, Dad, & Pom,

It sure was good to hear from you yesterday and to know that all of you was alright. I guess you are plenty tired now that berry season is on. They have a few berries over here in gardens, but it is too early for them now. The canned ones are good.

Dad, I guess you are getting plenty tired at the store, if there is no one to help you, and the rush is on as usual. I received a letter from Martha J. saying she was going to visit you, guess she is there by now.

I want you to send me thirty-five dollars. We got to buy a few things once in a while, and I owe some of the boys money that I have owed over a month. I will close for this time hoping to get your letter this afternoon.

Love, Porter

Kirchdorf, Austria
June 30, 1945

Dear Mom, Dad, & Pom,

It sure was good hearing from you today knowing that everyone was alright. Guess all of you are tired out by now if it has stopped raining long enough to work in the fields.

I'm fine as always and having a good time. We have been drilling all week and my platoon won over any other platoon in our company, yesterday we won over any other company in our battalion, today we won over any other battalion of our regiment so Tuesday we represent our regiment in competition against the rest of the division. We were playing softball late this afternoon and our drill Sgt. hurt his leg. We will be sure to lose if he isn't in because he is really good.

Hogs must really be high, you should have some for sale instead of buying. I'm hoping I can be there to help eat it this winter some time. I don't know anything about it if we will be there or not, just dreaming and hoping. I guess all of the Cornatzor family was glad to see Blake home. Did he and his wife stay in town or out at Mrs. Cornatzor's? What about Kenneth, did he join the Navy?

Pomvelle, don't you ever get a foolish idea like that in your head, unless the war is still going on when you are 18 then volunteer into some branch that you had rather be in and don't take the Infantry. Must close for this time, hoping to hear from you soon.

Love, Porter

Somewhere in Germany

May 8, 1945

Dear Mom, Dad & Pom,

It sure was good to hear from you yesterday, and to know that all of you was alright. I guess you are plenty tired now that berry season is on. They have a few berries over here in gardens but it is too early for them now. The canned ones are good.

Dad I guess you are getting plenty tired at the store, if there is no one to help you

The first page of Popo's letter from May 8th, 1945

and the rush is on as
usual.

I received a letter from
Martha J. saying she
was going to visit you
guess she is there by
now.

I want you to send
me thirty five dollars. We
get to buy a few things once
in a while and I owe
some of the boys money
that I have owed over a
month.

I will close for this
time hoping to get your letter
this afternoon.

Love,
Porter

The second page of Popo's letter from May 8th, 1945

As we were getting ready to leave, Popo looked at me, shook his head, and summed up all of his emotions, "I cannot understand war until this day. People are supposed to be more intelligent than that, more intelligent than to have to fight."

So that was Popo's war. He had been on the front line, in the middle of the combat. He had seen some of the most gruesome scenes of the war, the scenes that cause a man to awaken in the middle of the night fifty years later horrified, afraid, and haunted. Many of the pictures that his eyes beheld there on that European soil are images that must be driven into the farthest corners of his memory in order for him to come back and live an ordinary daily life. Popo experienced the horrors that lead one to pose deep questions about mankind and humanity. How can intelligent human beings subject one another to such unfathomable misery and horror? The "why's" and "wherefore's" of the war still weigh heavily on his mind.

What did Popo do when he returned? How did he deal with the haunting memories and questions? The only way he could. He locked them inside his heart, and he simply lived. He went back to Gadsden, Tennessee, back to farming, back to his family. He used the G.I. bill to take agriculture classes at the town high school. He knew more about farming than the teacher, but he received a monthly paycheck just for attending. He used the money to get married and begin his own life and family. He worked hard to provide a moderate income for his wife and three children. He watched his children grow up and have children of their own, but he always kept his wartime secrets tucked away. Was he trying to shield his family from the horrors? Were the memories simply too painful? Did he feel that no one else could understand? Whatever it was, and I would guess it to be a mixture of emotions, he has now broken that silence. There are still memories that lie deep within his soul that I suppose we will never know, but perhaps they are best left unknown.

What was it that caused him to finally speak? Was it the first time that someone had asked him about the war so directly? Was it the fact that it was his grandchildren's generation rather than his children's that was asking? Was it the weathering process that seems to happen through the years as memories are worn down by the sands of time? Or did he simply feel (as my father had said) the urgency of time, that if he was ever going to tell his story, he had to tell it now?

Does Popo feel better now that he has told the story? I would like to think he does, but I honestly cannot say. I am not sure that he knows. Talking about it is no magical cure. Perhaps it is a release, but perhaps it brings to life painful recollections that would have been better left in the distant corners of the memory. What I do know is that with his heartbreaking tears and with his gentle laughter, Popo told the story of his own personal war, so that his children, his grandchildren, and the world might know and understand.

Franz Josef von Laufenberg
March 30, 1915 - January 9, 1955

Chapter 2

Franz Josef: A Prisoner's Diary

I thought of all Germans as Hitler. That's all we heard about. We didn't hear nothing about German people that had any feelings or families.

I thought about what Popo had said about his view of the Germans and realized that my own picture of the German soldier was similar to what his had been. They were the hatred-filled, ruthless bad guys in all World War II films, the men who were supposed to be killed. Popo's picture of the German was forever altered when he heard a German describe his boyhood memories of the Hitler Youth; mine was destroyed when I read the diary of a German soldier.

The experience began when Georg and I were sitting in the stands of an isolated baseball field at Samford University one autumn night in 1999. We were just sitting there under the stars talking about everything that came into our minds: schoolwork, the future, our families. When we began talking about our families, I asked him for the first time what his grandfathers had done in World War II. He pondered the question for a moment and then replied, "I'm not sure exactly. I think they were both taken prisoner. One of them had a diary, I think. Omi [his grandmother] has tried to get us to type it before, but no one ever got around to it." I thought about that for a moment. A diary-unbelievable! I would love to read it; she definitely would not have to ask me twice to type it for her. I had no idea that two years later I would have the opportunity to do exactly that.

I went to Germany during June of 2000 in an effort to learn more about the wartime experiences of Georg's family members. When Georg's grandmother, whom her grandchildren call Omi, heard that I was interested in typing the diary, she was delighted. One morning she came over to Georg's house carrying the small, black, leather-bound book, along with photographs and newspaper clippings. We went upstairs to the computer, and she read the diary to me word-for-word, page-by-page as I typed. With each entry, I found myself more astounded by the poetic descriptions of Franz Josef's inner feelings. I was intrigued by his hopes and disappointments and amused by his perceptions and descriptions of America, my own homeland.

As I talked to Omi about the diary, I learned that her children and grandchildren had never read it. I was shocked. Everyone in my family listened intently to every word that Popo uttered about the war. When I had interviewed my grandfather, everyone had come into the room to listen. The room had been dead silent. On the other hand in Germany, none of Franz Josef's children or grandchildren had made time to type the diary (despite the repeated requests of Georg's grandmother). They were not able to read the journal because it had been written in Sütterlin script, an old form of German handwriting. Omi wanted to have the diary typed because she feared that when she passed away, the words of the diary would be lost forever.

Franz Josef von Laufenberg was born on March 30, 1915. He lived on a farm with his mother and sisters in Nörvenich, Germany. His father died in 1940, and as the oldest man on the farm, Franz Josef became the head of the household.

Because he was needed to support the family, he was not drafted until 1943 when he was 28 years old-much later than most young German men. After becoming an active soldier, he was captured almost immediately in Marseilles, France. After a brief stay in Africa, he was sent to America. There, he spent two years primarily doing farm work in several states. He was then sent to England, where he lived and worked for a farming family for another two years.

Franz Josef returned home in December 1947 and married Trude Hinzen in 1950. They had three children and were expecting another one (Georg's mother) when Franz Josef suddenly died. He was helping to remove a fallen tree after a storm when the tree fell and crushed his leg. While in the hospital recovering from a severely broken bone, he threw an embolism in his bone marrow and consequently died on January 9, 1955. He was only 39 years old.

Franz Josef began his diary with short, factual descriptions of what happened when, but as the years passed, his words serve as a testament to his own personal growth. As I typed Franz Josef's diary, I felt that I could see into the heart of this man. I felt as though I were there with him feeling his loneliness, yearning, and uncertainty. I regretted that I never had the opportunity to meet the man behind the poetic words and vivid descriptions. As I listened to Omi comment about her late husband and his writings, it was impossible to ignore the love and awe in her voice. They had only been married six years before his tragic death. She had lived without him for more than 45 years, yet the love and amazement that she felt toward this man had not diminished. And as I turned the last page of his diary and as Omi read the last sentence to me, I somehow felt as though I knew him as well. Following is a translation of the diary that Franz Josef von Laufenberg kept during his three-and-a-half year captivity.

Franz Josef with wife, on their wedding day, 1949

Franz Josef with his wife on their honeymoon

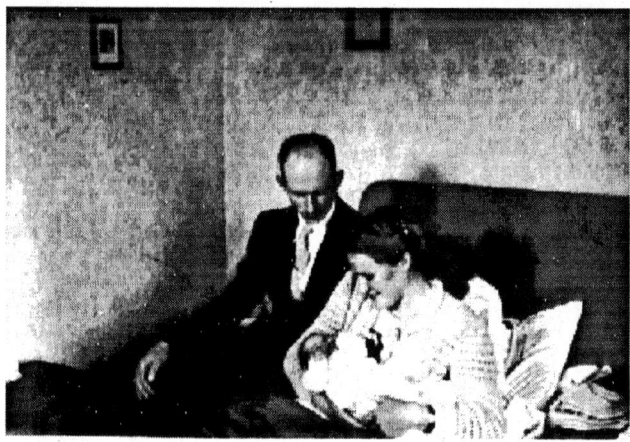

Franz Josef with his wife and their infant son Peter

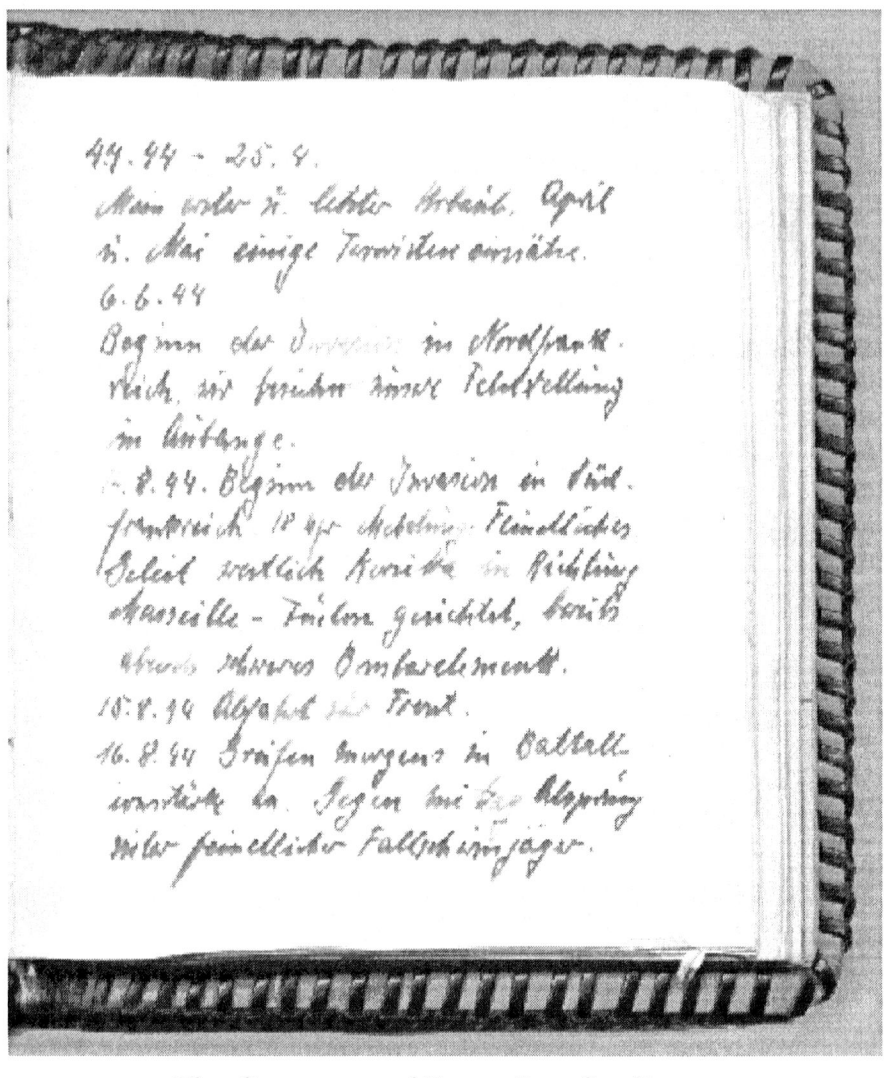

The first page of Franz Josef's diary

Journal from Captivity
Franz Josef von Laufenberg, Private First Class

If life leads you into lands afar, take your homeland with you in your heart.

April 4 - April 25, 1944: This was my first and last holiday leave. (I was stationed in Marseilles in the mountains of South France). There was some terrorist action in April and May.

June 6, 1944: The beginning of the invasion in northern France. We move into our field position in Auberge.

August 14, 1944: The beginning of the invasion in southern France. 6:00 P.M. report: Enemy escort, west Corsica in the direction of Marseilles...in the evening heavy bombardment.

August 15, 1944: Departure to the front

August 16, 1944: In the morning an attack on the battalion stronghold. Around noon many enemy paratroopers jump. Intense shelling, in which we have to give up our position. 7:30 A.M.: the enemy attacks after heavy drumfire. Due to so many losses we pull back to our starting position und there encounter that we are surrounded.

August 17, 1944: We try to break through with around 200 men. From 9:00 A.M. we are followed and hunted by the Americans who learn of our whereabouts through the betrayal of terrorists. In the evening due to a lack of water and heavy weapons we have to give ourselves up and go into captivity.

August 18, 1944: We are brought to a French port and are forced to work, loading ships and burying prisoners. We are treated well by the Americans, and the rationing is very good.

August 22, 1944: Board ship in the port of Maxim

August 23, 1944: Departure in the evening, destination still unknown. We travel with an escort of 18 ships and with some back-up boats.

August 28, 1944: Arrival in Oran. But we do not unload there; drive east to a small port. In the evening we leave the ship and board African boats. We are loaded directly into trucks and are taken to a large holding place in the interior "Nakura". I have a negative impression of Morocco. Large vineyards, their harvest is in full swing. Dust and sand, very hot, Moroccans very poor and dirty. Housing very poor - clay huts.

August 29, 1944: I send home my first letter from Africa.

August 30, 1944: Board ship in the port of Oran. It is supposed to go to America. We are happy that our stay in Africa was only a short one.

September 1, 1944: Around 2:00 in the morning we leave the port of Oran with a large escort of around 60-80 ships and many back-up vehicles.

September 2, 1944: We drive through the strait of Gibraltar; our last look at the European continent. We are on a freighter with 500 men, are fed with canned rations 3 times a day: one light, one heavy. The water is calm and the voyage bearable. During the day we are mostly on deck. Always the same picture, water and water. Mornings and evenings are the most beautiful. My thoughts are mostly about the homeland; from the front all kinds of rumors are coming through. V2 have supposedly been brought into action, the Russians brought to a standstill.

September 18, 1944: Finally after 18 days, arrival in Norfolk, North America

September 19, 1944: Leave the ship and are searched 4 times and then deloused. Our last possessions, that we had been able to sneak through until now, were taken from us. Now we have nothing more to remind us of the homeland than a torn and dirty suit. They immediately load us onto a train, and the journey into the unknown begins. We drive through Virginia, Ohio, Kentucky, Tennessee, Arkansas, Texas, New Mexico, and Arizona. We see completely new pictures, new life, new customs. My thoughts go instinctively to the Karl May years [Karl May is a popular German author who wrote fictitious novels about the "Wild West"], jungles, large cities with skyscrapers and again seemingly endless steppes with cattle. Then again fertile basins with corn, cotton, rice, and tobacco. In the middle of this wilderness, there are occasionally farmhouses. Mostly halfway fallen-in huts, all made from wood, just like the houses in the towns are mostly built out of wood. In front of the house is a car; every worker here owns one. The most beautiful limousines, and most all have a radio. We drive through towns and cities with the most magnificent neon signs, a whole lot of factories, and there are innumerable cars in the parking lots. Yeah, the closer we come to Texas, the larger the wilderness grows. We drive through wasteland for hours, occasionally seeing cowboys herding their cattle as they search for the sparse food.

September 23, 1944: Arrival in Florence, Arizona; we are given completely new clothes, a haircut, etc. The camp is very good with around 6000 men. We are treated and fed well.

September 29, 1944: We are put to work and have to pick cotton. We quickly spend our first paycheck in the delicious cafeteria.

[The following passage was written on a loose page and had been placed in the back of the journal. I include it here because of its chronological sequence.]

September 1944: Thoughts I would like to write down a few thoughts to you, my dear Gerta [his fiancé] and to you, my dear good Mother. Until now, I could send my thoughts to you in the homeland at my heart's desire, but today my hands are completely tied. What it means to me to be a Prisoner of War, that is "Kriegsgefangener," you know exactly. Even if we get good food here and are treated well, my thoughts of you loved ones and of the farm will not let go of me. I don't know anything more of you than of your love to me. Here we are hearing of bad fighting on the western front, from offenses until Düren. How are you, dear Gerta, you, dear Mother, and everyone? The uncertainty is hardly bearable. Only for a few hours did I have the privilege of defending the Fatherland against an overpowering of enemies. I saw many comrades fall and die, comrades, that also had a fiancé and even wives and children. War is hard and dreadful. It does not care who, how, or what someone is. Until now fate had spared me, but now the future lies before us dark and unknown. My belief in God and in our love gives me strength and hope. I know how you are worrying, and I want to hope that you have news about me. Unfortunately it will take a long time before I receive a greeting or even a sign of life from you. There were two king's children... I mean, Love, now the water is really too deep. [This is a reference to a famous German ballad.] But our love bridges everything, even the ocean, and for every parting there is a reunion. I have nothing anymore, no keepsakes, no pictures of you, only the change purse with the two grains of wheat from the Gymnishhof [the family farm] that I was able to sneak through until now. Did we not foresee at our last parting in Cologne-South [train station] that our separation would be a long one? A look, your look, was so sad but it also told me that everything would be O.K...no matter how lengthy the journey would be. In thought I am always with you in the homeland. What all have you lived through and what is still in front of you-you brides, wives, and mothers? The homeland in danger, the men on the front, or like me, in captivity and without news-uncertainty, fear, and worry. One often talks of heroes among us men, bestows us with high honors and medals, but you in the homeland remain without praise hymns and outer adornments. But there is none that would be sufficient for you. Does everything have to be this way? We ask ourselves over and over again: "Why?" What good is the fine food here, the good life? I am sitting in a golden cage. My heart and my mind are heavy and gloomy. I feel healthy and strong and cannot help you, can only watch as you suffer and sacrifice. Let us say with Christ, "O my Father, if it be possible, let this cup pass from me; nevertheless, not as I will but as thou wilt."

October 4, 1944: First letter sent home.

October 8, 1944: From the Red Cross, receive cigarettes and tobacco and black bread from the homeland. Worship service, card to Gerta.

A record of our food on Sunday, October 8, 1944:Breakfast: White bread, butter, hot chocolate

Noon: Pork riblets, potatoes, peas and carrots, apples, white bread, ground coffee.

Supper: White bread, pork sausage, liverwurst, cheese, and coffee

Now that I have been in Texas for 14 days, I want to write down my impressions. It has to be difficult for a European to move to this country. It's missing all the things that cause us to love the homeland: the dark forests, the fields with ever changing crops, the rivers and creeks, towns and cities. One must experience the tropics in order to treasure the German spring, summer, fall, and winter. And last but not least, the order and cleanliness and the good German customs. Here in Texas, that word says almost everything: endless steppes with little space between the brushwood and cacti, lifeless mountain ranges that remind one of a moonscape. The basins, with their many large cotton, rice and corn fields, can also only produce high yields by using artificial watering (electrical pumping devices). One can see well-fed herds of cattle on the large alfalfa fields and pastures. They are mostly red-colored and are only bred for fattening. There are warm-blooded horses, that you never see being used. You also see cowboys driving their herds back and forth along dry riverbeds. What I like the best are the riding saddles; they still come from the good old days and look just like the Wild West. There is no country where the motor has so changed the way of life as much as it has here. The hurry and rush have been transposed onto the people, they are always influenced by the speed of the machines. One could say that here the car shapes the way of life, and thus the cars are equipped with all kinds of luxuries. On the contrary, the houses remind me more of old robber dens than of the houses of civilized people. Our farmhands' homes are golden compared to them. The halfway fallen-in, dirty huts are sometimes made of clay and sometimes of boards. A halfway fallen-in car is almost always nearby. You only find nice clean houses in the towns, where the farmers also live. You don't see much game here, a few high-legged hares and more often big, large vultures that circle high in the hot air in search of a perished cow or horse, which they almost always find, as can be seen from the leftover bones. The engine has played a role in this area of life, too. The howling sirens of the "Texasese" remind me very much of the call of some kind of jungle monsters. The monotone noise of the airplane engines almost permanently fills the air. These engines have plenty of fuel due to the oil wells here that never dry up, whose towers can be seen from far away. They've already been here more than 25 years.

October 21, 1944: We have already been in another state, California, for three days. After a 24-hour train ride, we arrived here in good condition with 200 men. I thought we would now move on to another region but was terribly disappointed. There can only be one such barren desert. We have already driven about 150 km from our camp in a truck. During this whole stretch, we haven't seen anything living-no house, no animal, no tree, only mountains with a lot of sagebrush, not even a single green leaf. We are now in an American training camp and are supposed to be camp workers. We are housed in nice tents, beds with torn covers, etc. The food is also very good. During the day the temperature here is very hot and at night cold. I haven't heard anything in a long time from the homeland and still live in uncertainty about the fate of my loved ones.

October 28, 1944: Now that we have been here 10 days, I can once again put my ideas on paper. Because we still have not begun working and are being fed very well, it's almost going too well for us. We get a lot of meat, beef, pork, and mutton and even young chicken. Special holidays mean turkey, which here, like at home, is very valuable. Fruit everyday: apples, pears, grapes, pineapple, bananas, oranges, etc. Also a lot of eggs and cheese-like in a rest home. The only thing we have had to do until now is play Scat [a card game] and checkers. It would be a pleasure to work. There is nothing by way of agriculture here, only desolate wilderness. At night, the wolves come near our tents howling. The closest city is Los Angeles-150 km. We only hear bad news from the homeland. The Rhineland is supposedly evacuated, the Americans have begun shelling Cologne, the Russians are deep in East Prussia and have captured almost the entire Balkans. We are preoccupied with these thoughts all day. Where are all my loved ones? Mother, Gerta, Hedwig, Friedrich, Annemie, and Else. No prospect of news, even less of seeing the homeland again. What will the future bring? What sacrifices will still be demanded?

October 29, 1944: Worship service. A rainy Sunday. During the past few weeks various camp workers have performed. News from the homeland hasn't changed, fighting in Aachen, heavy air attacks, etc.

November 24, 1944: I am now busy with 8 other comrades in a kitchen and work there pretty much the whole day. The food has gotten better. In this regard things couldn't be any better. However, what good is all this when I think about what you are facing? Are you even at home? The never-ending thoughts and worries. The American newspaper records that Aachen, Geilenkirchen, Eschweiler have fallen, and the Americans are right in front of Düren. If I only knew something about where you are.

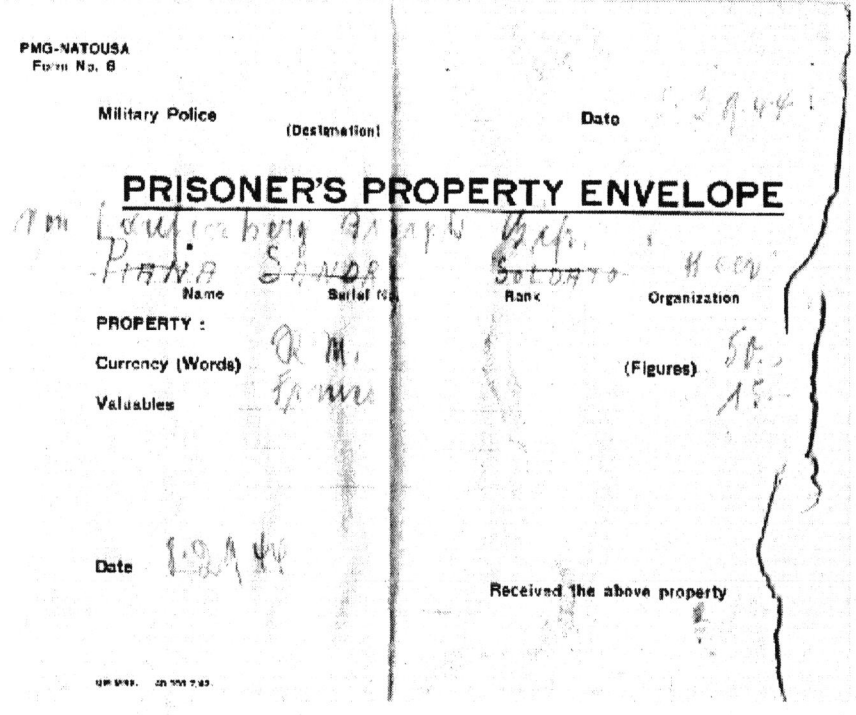

Envelope in which Franz Josef's valuables were stored during his captivity. He had 50 Reich marks and 15 French francs.

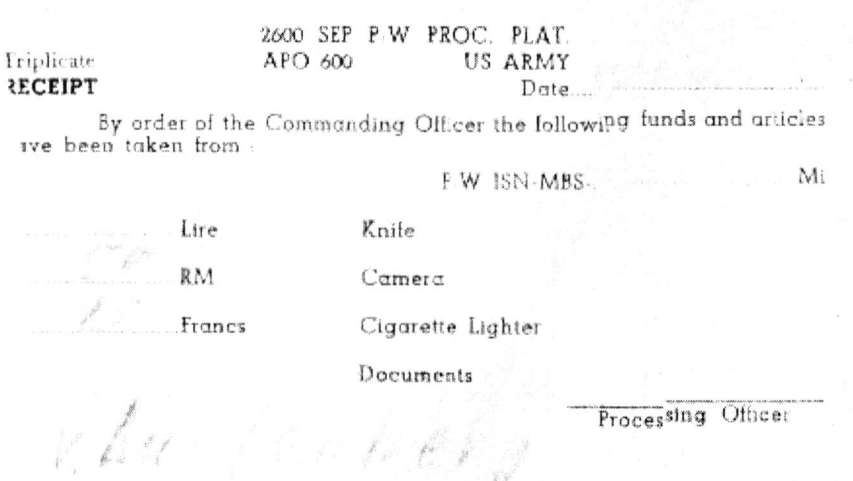

Receipt issued to Franz Josef listing
the valuables that were taken from him.

November 28, 1944: Letter sent home, card to Gerta.

December 1, 1944: One year ago today I learned of my fate.
Since then I have already experienced a great deal and got to
know life in three parts of the Earth, at least as well as possible,
as a soldier and a prisoner. When I consider that one year ago
I was still at home on our farm with all my loved ones! Despite
the war, they were still wonderful times that I was allowed to
spend with you, my loved ones. Above all, I had planned to
spend many happy hours with you, dear Mother. Only here
in a foreign country have I first realized how much you mean
to me, dear Mother, and how valuable you are. Every evening
I pray to our Lord God and ask him to keep you healthy for a

long time. A great sacrifice is also demanded of you, dear Gerta. One blow brought all of our dreams and plans to nothing. Life is hard and relentless. We have to wait and hope and not know if and when our desire will again become reality. We ask our Lord God daily to allow our wish to come true.

December 10, 1944: Do you think, dear Gerta, that one year ago today in Osnabrück, we thought that everything would happen the way it has? Letters sent home and to Gerta.

December 16, 1944: Today, dear Gerta, my thoughts center completely on you. Which birthday will you have celebrated before our wedding?

December 24, 1944: Christmas Eve. We had a very nice Christmas celebration here in the Californian desert, very much German style. Naturally only with thoughts of you, loved ones at home, and of the wonderful Christmas celebrations of our childhood when our good father was still with us. Letter to Gerta.

January 1, 1945: Turn of the year. We live with the hope that the New Year will permit the coming of new peace and new happiness. That is the desire of the whole world.

Franz Josef after the war

January 5, 1945: Letter sent home.

January 6, 1945: Today I want to give a detailed description of the American soldier. Compared to us, he is for the most part considerate and courteous. His life is much less complicated and freer than that of the Germans. He says, first a man then a soldier; with us it was completely backwards. America seems to be overflowing with food. They only eat the best and the finest; everything else is thrown in the garbage. On top of that, the soldiers do not have to do as much as those in Germany. I've also met many who speak German and many whose parents and grandparents sailed over from the homeland. Almost all of them believe that life here is considerably easier than at home in Germany. For example, a Bavarian, who emigrated in 1931 and had a small store at home, bought a few acres of land here for 5 dollars an acre, cleared it himself, and now has 25 cows, all modern machinery, a car, etc. and is a farmer. Here everybody can become whatever occupation they choose. The only thing they are missing is the German contentment, the peace and quiet, and the family life, the German way of life and customs. Also, maybe it is the tough struggle for daily bread and the worries that allow us to love the fatherland. In comparison, the motto here is "Earn a lot and spend a lot." Another notable thing is that here the man is not the deciding factor but rather the woman. If he has torn pants, she has at least a fur coat and finger- and toenails in the loudest shimmering colors, regardless of age, and everywhere the inevitable cigarette in their mouths, if they're 20 or 60 it doesn't matter. The man is just working for the amusement of his wife.

February 4, 1945: It has already been 5 years now since our

father left us, and his life, which served only his family, the farm, and above all the future of his children, had to end so early. Maybe it was God's will that his sacrifices and suffering not be made greater by this terrible war. Our remembering him just serves as reverence and thankfulness to him.

February 17, 1945: Six months in captivity. The hopes that the war would be over by now have not been fulfilled. What if the war still does not end this year?

March 2, 1945: Today I read a newspaper again that said that the homeland is now in American hands. The Amis have supposedly made it to Mödrath, so not far from Cologne. If I only knew now, if you all are still in Nörvenich and if the farm is still standing, then I would not need to worry so much. Hope to receive mail from you soon and to find out the details from and about you. Most of my comrades have already received mail.

March 17, 1945: Today my thoughts are especially on you, dear Gerta and I send you my warmest regards on your Saint's Day [a day celebrated in honor of the saint after whom a person was named; in the past it was considered more important than a person's birthday in Germany].

March 30, 1945: Am now 30 years old and would have rather celebrated my birthday somewhere else besides here in America.

April 1, 1945: Easter, we don't notice the holidays much here and hope that this is the last one as a prisoner. Spring has also come here in the desert. Despite the dryness, the shrubs are becoming green, and here and there you can see some flowers. By the way, the area here is barren just like before.

April 7, 1945: We again leave our base and travel 130 miles farther to Camp Haan, a larger training camp, where we will also be used as camp workers. We travel by truck, and halfway there we again see large cacti and later also some deciduous and conifer trees, come to a large orange plantation and even pass barley and oat fields. All around are high mountains that still have snow-covered peaks. You could almost believe that you were in the Alps. Life goes on here in the camp, just like in the last one. The work is not any better. Among the newly-arriving comrades, I have met some from near home, from Arnoldsweiler, Düren, Schleiden, and one from Kreuzau, whose grandparents are Johannes Keller from Nörvenich. They are supposedly living in Lechenich because their house was destroyed.

May 3, 1945: Our stay in Camp Haan should not last long either. We are already leaving again today. We are on a train headed north, again hours and hours through a desolate, mountainous area. After a 24-hour train ride we are unloaded in a main camp in Stockton, a small port 100 km from the Pacific coast. Here we are split up and are transported further by trucks. Again we see completely new things, vast pastureland with good herds of livestock and huge wheat fields. Later we see vegetable fields, one after the other. Finally there's something living again in nature.

May 5, 1945: After arriving in our camp, our first job is to set up the tents. Here everything is flat, as far as the eye can see.

May 7, 1945: Today may be the most eventful day of our captivity. The American army told us that the German troops have stopped fighting and that the German government no longer exists. The war is over. What that means for us is easy to understand. The suffering and sacrifice of the homeland has stopped, and the murdering and slaughtering has come to a definite end. If now all the blood has flowed in vain, it's good that it's over because a good ending was no longer possible. We can hardly think about how the homeland must look now, and sad, grim news awaits almost all of us. How does it look for you loved ones on the farm? Are you all still alive? Are you still healthy, and are at least parts of the buildings still standing? In the past few days, I got a picture of Düren, which the Americans captured on February 23. I saw the Bismarck memorial unscathed; the surrounding houses, however, were all heaps of rubble. I hope that I find out at least somewhat good news and above all that I can soon go home.

May 8, 1945: For work we are chopping sugar beets, exactly like at home, except here everything is already further along. Here you only see tractors in the fields. The plots of land are almost all more than 100 Morgen [ca. 62 acres] big.

June 4, 1945: The war has been over now for almost a month, and we still haven't heard anything about the homeland or about you loved ones. We are also completely unsure as to what our lot is to be. From the rubble field of Germany, it seems that the victors are chasing the leaders from one conference to another to divide the last few remnants. From the homeland itself, we are hearing of famine and revolts. What you all have to go through! When will there finally be peace and quiet? Because I have now been here four weeks, I want to report briefly about some of the local farming methods. As I've already said, all the plowing here is done with tractors and with large caterpillars. For the easier work, they put rubber tires on the machines, and they don't plow too deeply but always in circles. Then they work with a tractor and Wehe [a piece of farming equipment that was pulled behind the tractor that is generally no longer used], and the hoeing machine is attached underneath the tractor, in order to spare people and materials. When the sugar beets are hoed for the last time, a case of fertilizer is installed above the shares so that the fertilizer goes directly onto the roots. The pests are eradicated with small airplanes that spray the fields. The motto here is "Speed, Speed!" Most farmers here have 5000 Morgen [ca. 3090 Acres] and even more. They grow sugar beets, onions, asparagus, but they cut it when it is still only green, right above the ground [in Germany they waited until it turned somewhat white], peas, and a lot of tomatoes, lettuce, and carrots, but only for the seeds. Here they still grow a lot of alfalfa but only to grind it up and dry it-up to 6 times a year. Mexicans do most of the work that has to be done by hand and everything is done in rhythm. Sprinkler systems are used in the fields day and night.

June 17, 1945: We have already been in captivity for 10 months, and I had my first opportunity to go to the Holy Sacraments. A priest that comes from Hall, near Innsbruck, read the Mass. We hear new rumors concerning our trip home everyday. According to the latest one, the oldest (based on age) prisoners will be freed in August. We hope that that is true and that I will be among them. My biggest worry is still the uncertainty of your fate. How can I find out everything?

Das einzige bis jetzt bekannte Bild von den Kampfhandlungen in der Stadt Düren am 25. 2. 1945 wurde von einem amerikanischen Kriegsberichterstatter gemacht und nahm damals seine Runde durch die ganze Weltpresse. Seine traurige Berühmtheit verdankt es nicht zuletzt der einem amerikanischen Journalisten von einem in Düren verbliebenen Zivilisten gemachten Bemerkung, daß die Denkmalfigur des Fürsten Bismarck in der Bismarckstraße (unsere Aufnahme) durch das Bombardement und den Artilleriebeschuß eine Drehung um 180 Grad gemacht habe. Darüber heißt es in einer amerikanischen Soldatenzeitung "Bismarck blickt zum Rhein. Ursprünglich schaute die eherne Statue nach Frankreich und Belgien. Aber nach zwei Nächten Bombardement hatte sich die Figur völlig rundgedreht, so daß Bismarck, wie alle Deutschen, jetzt zum Rhein blickt". Diese Feststellung beruht, wie auf dem Bild deutlich zu sehen ist, auf einem Irrtum. Bismarck blickte auch nach dem fürchterlichen Bombardement nach wie vor zum Westen. Die Figur hatte nur einen auf der Aufnahme deutlich zu erkennenden kleinen Ruck nach rechts gemacht . . .

The above article appeared in a German newspaper on February 15, 1955, ten years after the war and six weeks after Franz Josef's death. This is probably the picture that Franz Josef saw while he was in captivity. The text underneath reads, "The only picture known to date depicting the fighting in the city of Düren. It was taken by an American war correspondent, and it later circulated through the worldwide press. Its heartbreaking renown can be much credited to the comment that was made to an American journalist (by a civilian that stayed in Düren) stating that the Bismarck statue had made a 180-degree turn due to the bombardment and artillery fire. According to one military newspaper, 'Bismarck looks at the Rhine. Originally the iron ore statue faced France and Belgium. But after two months of bombardment, the figure completely turned around, so that Bismarck, like all Germans, now looks towards the Rhine.' This claim, as apparent from the picture, was an error. Even after the terrible bombardment, Bismarck still faces west. The photo clearly shows only a slight turn to the right."

July 4, 1945: Today after 10 months my pictures came back. Now I hope that mail from the homeland arrives soon. After having chopped sugar beets for 6 weeks now with 16 men per farmer, we have now begun the pear harvest. Of course, here everything is also done in a certain rhythm and in record time. We started with 20 crates, 50 pounds each, per day, and are now picking 45.

July 15, 1945: After the many rumors, we can now supposedly count on returning home at the end of the year. But these are only rumors to which we cling. From the homeland itself, we hear only bad news, and the victors still cannot agree about the future of Europe. The French will supposedly take possession of the region left of the Rhine.

August 14, 1945: The pear picking has now finally stopped after 5 weeks with 60 men. Tomorrow we are supposed to start with the onions.

August 17, 1945: Now we have been prisoners of war for almost a whole year and still have no news from you loved ones in the homeland. According to the latest news from the newspapers, the English will now possess our region. In the cities the food supply is supposedly very short. Maybe after there is also peace with Japan, everything will go faster, and we will even be able go home soon. This week I had the opportunity to talk with our farmer, and he said that he, along with 3 other brothers, manages 4000 Acres (that's around 8000 Morgen) with 17 tractors and in the summer months around 250 outside helpers, mainly Mexicans. That is around 2000 - 3000 Morgen of sugar beets which yield 20 tons per acre without natural fertilizer but with about the same artificial fertilizer that we use in Germany. Because it hasn't rained a drop from May 8 until today, the sprinkler systems have to run day and night. In addition, he cultivates a lot of tomatoes, asparagus, onions, lettuce, and string beans and some barley along with that. Along the canal he has large pear orchards that yield a good crop. His fortune is estimated to be around 4,000,000 dollars.

September 2, 1945: Met a comrade in the past few days from the Erkelenzer area, who was captured in May in Honnef. He was transported by truck through Euskirchen, Zülpich, Düren, to Aachen. He says that there is hardly a house left undamaged in Düren but that the surrounding places were pretty much spared. Otherwise you don't hear much new, and most of that is made up.

September 9, 1945: It is Sunday again, and I have a lot of time to dwell on my thoughts of you loved ones in the homeland. Again and again the same question: Are you all still alive and is the farm still there? When and how will I ever find you all again? Here we learn about everything from the newspapers we get from the homeland. Food is supposedly still very tight, still no mail and no train connection. Supposedly the worst hit are the inhabitants of the eastern regions. There is another rumor here that we should be home by Christmas. We can only hope. If that were true, I would not even need to rely on mail anymore. We have now finished working in the onions for our farmer. We had around 80 men and each man pulled out and sacked 30 Ctr [65 lbs] per day. Beginning tomorrow, we should begin work in the sugar beets, where we only need to pull out the bad ones. The machines do everything else. It pulls the sugar beet out, a circle that is around 180 cm [70 inches] big that has spikes on it raises the sugar beet up, where it's cut and then falls on a conveyor belt and is then transported onto a truck driving next to it. These two-tiered machines can harvest around 15 Morgen [9 acres] a day. They leave the leaves in the fields as food for sheep or cattle.

October 7, 1945: It rained today for the first time in 5 months. At least we don't have to pick any tomatoes today, which we have already been harvesting now for 3 weeks. Our farmer has around 500 morgen [300 acres] of tomatoes and harvests 80 Ctr. per morgen [16 tons per acre]. We have to pick around 45 crates daily, that is around 22 Ztr. [2 tons]. Besides that, our life here is primitive. One day just like the other: eat, work, and sleep. The only changes in the routine are the Sunday worship service and a movie once a week. Of course, our hope of going home soon is ever present, but many fears and worries are also associated with that because I and many comrades still don't have any news; some have good, others only bad. After 6 months of not being allowed to send a letter home, we recently heard that we might be able to in the upcoming weeks. For me it no longer seems possible that you can write letters and find out about loved ones. When you wait again and again in vain, you soon completely give up hope. How only a word from you, dear Mother, could make my life here easier and free me from many hours of gloominess. I know that when we come home, all our strength will be needed there, and that we cannot allow ourselves to hang our heads. If only all of you loved ones are still healthy, I will not be afraid of the future. The only thing I have left is the comfort and consolation of prayer.

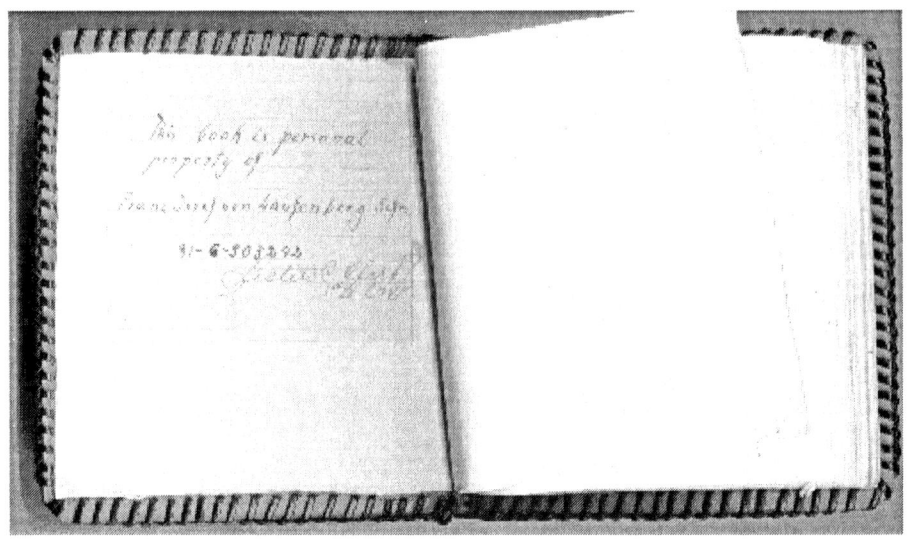

The inside cover of Franz Josef's diary

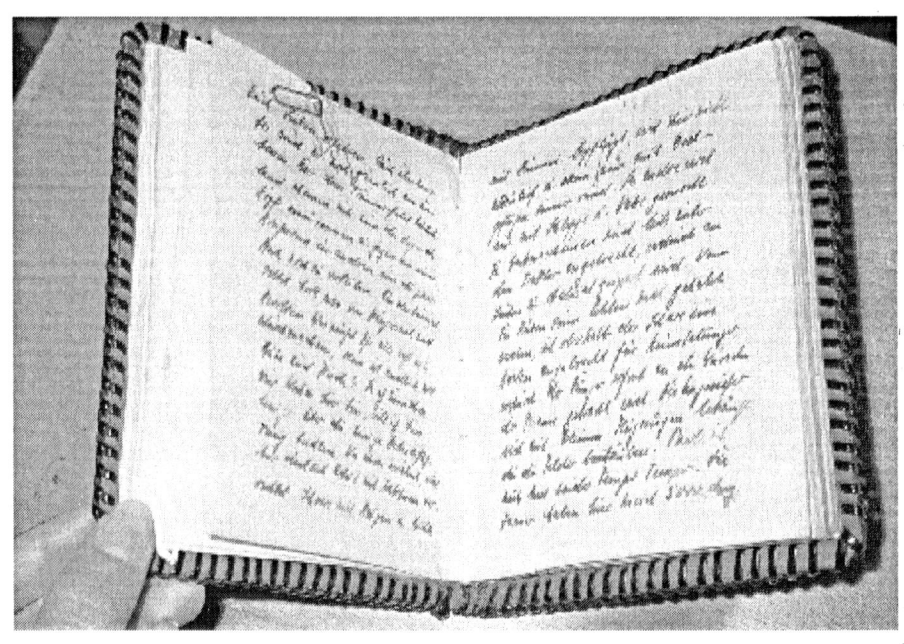

Pages of Franz Josef's diary

October 16, 1945: We have now already been harvesting for several weeks, and it will still take 4-5 more weeks. In the meantime it is autumn, and it is already becoming fairly cool. What will happen to us then - home or another new workplace? The worries remain, just as they do at home. Supposedly at home there is a large food and coal shortage. In Cologne Adenauer von Fuchs has supposedly been named Lord Mayor. I repeat the same question over and over: How are you all?

November 3, 1945: Finally another letter sent home, airmail over Genf with reply. Hopefully I will now receive news from you soon. Now we are working in the "Füdderrüben" [beets used as animal feed]. The harvests are good here in California, and it is understandable why they call it the "Golden State."

December 3, 1945: [new camp] Here you only see huge pastures, steppes, and cotton fields. The dairy cattle seem to be in poor condition, but the beef cattle look good. We are in the cotton harvest and are supposed to pick 2 Ztr. (220 pounds) a day. We are here in Clarksburg, and the soil is very sandy. You can see from the buildings and machines that this is not a good area. The Americans don't place a lot of value on order and cleanliness. Our camp is near a large mountain range that is always covered with snow and that separates us from the Pacific coast.

December 24, 1945: Filled with magic and secrecy for children, the blissful, dreamlike time draws near again. [a quote from a German Christmas poem] This is probably the hardest Christmas that you loved ones in the homeland and we here will have to experience-so far, far away from you. It is almost midnight, and I am coming back from our district communal celebration. There were 700 comrades there, all of whom share the same fate. It is true that my thoughts are with you at home, with you dear Mother, Gerta, and everyone. I think back on the years of our childhood when our father was still with us; he always made everything especially festive. I think on the unforgettable hours of our childhood, on the magic and the bliss that the Christkind [literally, the "Christ child" who supposedly brings the Christmas presents to the children in Germany instead of Santa Claus] brought to us through you, dear parents. If my anxious thoughts reach you tonight, I hope that you, dear Mother, at least have Friedrich, Hedwig, Elschen, und Annemie with you and that they help you to bear this heavy burden. Now almost one and a half years have passed since I received the last news from you. The only means of connection with you are the thoughts that are in these hours especially filled with longing and love for you. If only it would soon be over, the eternal hoping, waiting, and fearing. If only I might soon be with you again. When and how? These thoughts and questions are filled with uncertainty and emptiness. Everything lies so very far back but also so near. Whom will I see again; whom will I not see? How does the farm look? Maybe the way that I left it. I think about Rose [the family's horse] who did her duty for over 20 years loyally and unselfishly. I think about both of the studs, about the fields and buildings. How beautiful it used to be in the homeland and how will it be and become?

January 1, 1946: A whole year has now gone by, a year that brought the end of the war but everything but the peace that had been hoped for and the calm that had been longed for. At the moment, the homeland is struggling through the most misery and poverty in its history, and the hope for a better future is only very bleak.

January 10, 1946: Now it seems true that they will send us home soon. By April all POW's should be out of America. Our contract runs out on January 30, and we supposedly will not begin a new job. My hopes are high, but my feelings are mixed. I would leave here without any news from you and would first there encounter whatever awaits me. I pray God that this reunion will be the happiest day of my life.

February 10, 1946: For 10 days we have been in a new camp not far from the last one and are again picking cotton and have 1000 men per farmer on one lot. This field is that big, and after the harvest the land will be worked again with 7 tractors. Yesterday my friend received a card from October 1945 with news that everyone is healthy. Then I met a comrade from Kerpen, Heinrich Möll, who was in captivity even before Africa and who has also not received any news. We are now living in great suspense and are still waiting and hoping.

February 27, 1946: Today I finally received the so long awaited mail from you. My joy is overflowing, and I can hardly wait for the day when I will see you all again. I thank God that you are all healthy; everything else can be rebuilt.

March 13, 1946: No godly person is enjoying undivided joy. [an alteration of a line taken from Friedrich von Schiller's poem "Polycrates' Ring," which states that "No earthly person is enjoying undivided joy."] Our hopes were again betrayed. We had awaited our trip home and our release with certainty, and then shortly before departure, everything blew up again. My disappointment and mood are beyond description. Then on top of that, I also had the tough luck of being the only one of the comrades, whom I had known since France, to be put into a neighboring camp. I can no longer find pleasure here in America. On March 9, I again received a card from you, and I hope now that the mail from you will continue to come. I learned from a comrade from Düren that the Dürener [a family they knew from the town of Düren] were still alive but that Gertraud was killed in a bombing raid. I thank our Lord God that he has kept you for us, dear Mother, and has not demanded a sacrifice from you. If the many worries about you loved ones has now subsided, then the longing and yearning for all of you loved ones in the homeland has intensified.

March 17, 1946: This time, my dear Gerta, I still have to send you my Saint's day regards in thought. They should therefore be especially sincere; my wishes and hopes are yours, would like for them to come true soon.

March 27, 1946: I finally received my first letter from you, dear Gerta, and I am happy that you are also doing well and that you are still healthy. The letters were from November of the past year, and I have to presume that you went a whole year with no news from me. It is very painful for me to find out that our house is destroyed, and I can't imagine where you all are staying.

March 28, 1946: All of our hopes were crushed again today. We're going to Clarksburg again to work on the farm, and it will probably last until fall. Our hopes are crushed again and again. The newspapers from the homeland are spreading rumors that we are staying here voluntarily and don't want to go home. I hope that no one believes this fraud. I would be deceiving myself if I said that I had been satisfied or happy one minute in captivity.

April 17, 1946: Luckily our farm work only lasted 14 days, and today we, along with 700 other men from the English zone, returned to our previous camp. We don't know what will happen now.

April 16 [26], 1946: Today I could send mail home again after one year and a package to Genf, Number 79126, a letter to Gerta's home

May 1, 1946: We are still in Letrop, turned in our work clothes, and they are talking about our discharge. We should go to England.

May 7, 1946: We, along with 900 men (out of the English zone), rode the train towards New York. It is the same journey as before, and we see the same pictures that we saw one and a half years ago. Prosperity and poverty, wilderness and culture change along with the terrain, the climate, and the population. The Mississippi had high water this time, and after a 5-day train trip we arrived on May 13 in the shipping yard near New York. Here there are 15,000 men from every zone that are waiting to board the ship and go home.

May 17, 1946: It's getting serious, and we are loaded onto a troop transporter in New York, along with 2000 men. At 9:00 in the evening we set out without knowing the destination of our journey. We see the New York metropolis with its skyscrapers, a labyrinth of ports on both sides. It is an overwhelming sight, the brightly illuminated masses of stone, hundreds of stories rising high in the dark night sky.

May 18, 1946: We learn while at sea that we are going to Liverpool and will be unloaded there. There we have to wait and see what the English plan to do with us. The ocean crossing is nothing particular, and we are happy to have solid ground under our feet again in Liverpool. Many were seasick.

May 28, 1946: We started in Liverpool and traveled by train to a large camp in Nottingham. Again our hopes and prospects amounted to nothing because we will have to work again here. I lack the words to write down what I'm feeling right now.

June 1, 1946: We saw an operetta today ("Feuersauber der Liebe"), that was conducted by some fellow soldiers and that we liked a great deal.

June 9, 1946: It is Pentecost, and a worship service is our only reminder of that. Our hopes to go home were futile.

June 14, 1946: We are transferred from the big camp to Plympton, South England. Here they organize us for construction work, and we build living quarters out of cement blocks. Now I can write mail more often...to Mother, Gerta, and to relatives. I have traveled through many countries and have seen a good piece of the earth on my involuntary trip around the world. Though it was very hard for me to forget my lot and fate during these hours and days, I had to do it in order to take in the pictures without prejudice. Even if every continent and every country attracts me in different ways, I have discovered that every country has its beauty. Be it the Riviera of southern France, the hot sand deserts of Morocco, the many states with their ever-changing landscapes of America, or the hilly pasturelands of England. One need be neither an author nor poet to be impressed by the newness everywhere. It's almost exactly the same with people as with such things, because I meet them without any prejudices and without any hatred, and I am seldom disappointed. Be it with whites or blacks, Mexicans or Jews, which through some kind of seditious campaign believed that they had to hate us, most of them were after a short time the most understanding and the most thoughtful of people. I have already been in England 4 weeks and unfortunately still have no prospect of discharge and trip home. I find it difficult to hold my head high and to keep searching again and again for the desire to hope for the future. If the sun rises here the same time it does where you are and the distance to you is much shorter, my longing and yearning to be with you has intensified that much more. From the homeland we hear only bad news: famine in the big cities, and above all the newspaper reports of 18 political parties, etc. However, about peace and order, the most important matters, we hear nothing. Poor Germany!

July 15, 1946: The mail is coming more often, and I find out from a letter from Annemie and Heinrich how you all look and what all you have lived through. If I could only be with you! It's a huge relief to be able to keep constant contact with you through letters. Maybe it is the fate of Gymnischhof [the name of the family farm] to stand as a constant fight for existence. It was our dear father's life's work to keep the farm going. Unfortunately he had to leave us all too soon-just as the success of his hard, tireless worry was guaranteed. For 3 years I, with everyone else's help, was granted the privilege of carrying on the work that Father had begun, but then the plow was also taken from my hand. For almost two years now the responsibility has almost without exception been on the shoulders of our Hedwig [his sister]. If you, dear Sister, leave us now, we will all know that wherever you may be, you will always remain a child of Gymnischhof, and this person, for one, will always know, how much he has to thank you for. We can thank our Lord God that we all came through this pointless war without bodily harm. When I return, it will be a joy for me, along with Friedrich, to take care of our dear Mother and everyone. If the farm is not capable of producing any material goods in the foreseen future, we still want to keep it open for you all, so that it may always be your home.

August 30, 1946: Already 3 months in British captivity and still no prospect of being set free. It is superfluous to ponder about the "why's" and "wherefore's" because no one can give a legitimate answer. When you consider that millions of people are starving and just as many are without work, others carrying out unproductive work, then one's own situation does not seem so bad. If this happens in the age of our illustrious culture and the atomic bomb, I am thankful for all the magic. We've already been at a new place in Plymouth for 5 weeks. It is very nice here on the coast. At night we see the sailboats and yachts crossing along the hilly coast. We were also led through the spa in the accompaniment of a guard. You feel like an outsider when you see the lives of free people. They're talking about allowing us to go out by ourselves for two hours each day, but we will be allowed neither to talk to civilians nor to go into a house. They can offer me what they want, but I will never be happy here and will always only wait for the day I can go home.

Franz Josef's widow (left) visits the Hoskin's, the English family for whom Franz Josef worked. Despite the early death of Franz Josef, the two families have kept in contact with one another since the war.

The Hoskin's visit Franz Josef's family, who still live at Gymnischhof. This picture shows the Hoskin's (middle) with Franz Josef's son Peter and grandson Bernd.

September 2, 1946: Began my work on a farm today. Completely live here and am treated well-as part of the family.

September 18, 1946: Now the British government is also occupying itself with the release of the prisoners. According to the last publication, all prisoners should be back within 18 months. Naturally I hope that I am not among the last. I have been on the farm for almost 3 weeks now and am happy that I took on this position. I have more freedom and don't have barbed wire in front of me anymore. My boss, Mr. Hoskin, has a cattle farm and 40 cows (red-colored south Devon Rene) all English longhorns. I am the only worker except for him. I have to help with milking and all the work. So far I am treated as one of the family, sometimes like a silent partner. The buildings are very old, all made of stone fragments but have held up well. The house where they live reminds me very much of Old England: an open fire, very good old fireplace. The cooking is done over the open fire. Electric light, etc. are completely nonexistent. The people live very well, and I experience new surprises daily at meal times. 6:30 is wake-up. Afterwards, the cows must be brought in from the pasture, and we begin immediately with the milking. At 9:00 the stalls are ready and then we have the first breakfast, consisting mostly of fried eggs, fried potatoes, bread, cream, and cake, which is not missing from any meal. Then we do some field or farm work. 1:15 is lunch. At 5:00 is tea, then we work some more in the stalls until 7:00. At 9:00 is supper. They cook relatively little, mostly only potatoes, and they eat the peeling. Nothing is spared when it comes to fats, meat, and cake. Naturally there is only tea in England, rarely hot chocolate and even more rarely coffee.

August - October: various mail sent home and to Gerta

October 15, 1946: After receiving only a few letters from my fiancé this past half year in England and those only full of complaints and accusations, I have decided to put an end to our relationship. I do not want to get out of prison here in order to enter into another one. I again grew richer from an experience and a disappointment.

Many letter exchanges

October 2, 1946?: Was taken tonight to the main camp for political questioning and hope that this is another step closer to home. But I have come to terms with them until spring. I don't find it so difficult anymore because I know you at

home are in the best of condition. At the farm I am still in the best of situations. I am allowed to take part in everything, in the cow market, farming positions, etc. Of course, life is easiest for me when I am working, and that is most of the day.

Again, many letter exchanges

December 24, 1946: I spent this Christmas Eve alone at the farm. Unlike the last two years, I know the situation of all my loved ones, and the oppressing feeling of uncertainty, thank God, has been alleviated. They celebrate Christmas here in England like they do in America: they decorate the Christmas tree with paper ornaments, and good food is supposed to bring in the spirit.

January 1, 1947: Celebrated New Year's Eve here at the farm

but only with the usual apple juice. My biggest comfort is knowing that this is the last time I will have to spend this holiday in a foreign country. Otherwise, I'm doing very well here at the farm. However, one is still a prisoner and enjoys pleasure only based on the work accomplished. I am always looking forward to good news from home and am in thought almost constantly with you loved ones at home.

Easter, 1947: Had the opportunity to attend a worship service again today. Otherwise didn't notice much of the Easter spirit. Overall, Sundays are not observed here the way they are at home. We always work until noon and at 4:00 everything starts again with the milking and work. I have not written much [in my journal] during the past 14 months and am constantly busy. It would also have been superfluous because of the constant letter exchange with you. Today I finally found out the day of my release. I should leave this camp on December 3 and on December 7 board a ship toward home. All of my wishes and hopes during the last years should finally come true; it is still hard to grasp and to believe. I hardly know what it means to be free. To be together with all of my loved ones and to be able to work on the place that I call and will forever call home. When I think back, everything, despite the worry and fear, will be good again in the long run, and when I see everyone again, may I know that it is the old homeland, my homeland, that will take me back again.

With those words of hope, Franz Josef von Laufenberg ended the journal he kept through his years as a prisoner of war. It seems that although he was involved in one bloody battle, the gruesome combat was not his greatest wartime struggle. Rather his toughest battle was the one he faced everyday inside his heart. He lived in a world of loneliness, uncertainty, and disappointment. He lived eighteen months without knowing whether his family and friends were alive or dead and without knowing if he had a home to which he could return. He began hoping that he would be freed the moment the war was over in May of 1945 but faced one disappointment after another before finally returning home in December of 1947.

Franz Josef's journal makes it clear how dear his family was to him, yet he was forced to be away from them for five years. I only wish that I had record of their reunion. Was there unspeakable joy? Did they hug and laugh and cry? Or did they feel more like strangers, as though they had known one another in a past life, a life before the terrible war? How many days or months or years did it take before home felt like home again?

Franz Josef had ended his diary with the statement, "May I know that it is the old homeland, my homeland that will take me back again." I wondered about that statement. What had Franz Josef found when he returned? Was he able to recognize his old homeland in a Germany left destroyed and ashamed by the war? And perhaps the more important question and the one more difficult to answer, had his homeland taken him back again? He had been a soldier, a Nazi soldier. He was no different than Popo in the fact that he had been drafted and forced to serve. Yet there was a major difference. Popo's army had won. They returned home heroes that had upheld democracy, liberty, and human rights. They were praised for defending their country and the world against tyranny. Franz Josef's army had lost. They had fought for the Führer's goal of a Groß-Deutschland. They had battled to defend a totalitarian state. What did that make Franz Josef?

In his journal Franz Josef never commented on his thoughts about Hitler or the Nazi party; he never even mentioned the words. His deep, often religious thoughts and his openness to other people and other cultures seemed to stand in stark contrast to the brutal Nazi tyrants that I had always seen portrayed in films. I do not wish to say that there were no such German soldiers; the atrocities committed during the war prove otherwise. However, by reading Franz Josef's diary, I met a real German soldier, a man whose love for his family was greater than his love for his Fatherland and who voiced the German culture through quotes from Schiller rather than from Hitler.

Franz Josef had been much like Popo, a young man taken away from his home, his family, and the life that he knew and sent to fight in a terrible war. When Popo returned, he had not talked about the war due to the terrible scenes that he had witnessed. What had Franz Josef done when he had returned? How had he felt? Did he talk about his experiences or did he, too, try to forget the past? Had he felt guilty or ashamed? Was he angry about having lost five years of his life? How would the last fifty years have altered his memories of the war? What would he think if he knew that his grandson's wife, an American, was one of the first people to ever read his wartime diary? These are only a few of the questions that can never be answered.

Another question that intrigued me was whether or not Franz Josef's and Popo's paths may have ever crossed during the war. Popo's first question to my husband had been, "Did your grandfather steal my Christmas present?" Of course, the chance that either of Georg's grandfathers had actually been among that small group of German soldiers was unimaginably slim, but was it possible that they had seen one another at some point in time? Was it possible that they had ever caught one another's eye for even a moment?

Franz Josef was in captivity in the United States before Popo ever left for Europe. In September 1944 Franz Josef described the train ride across the country from Virginia to Arizona; he lists the states the train traversed on its long journey. Among those states was Tennessee. A train track runs through downtown Gadsden, near the cotton gin and near Popo's farm. Was this the path that Franz Josef had taken? Did he look out the train window and see the wooden farmhouse and the cotton fields? Were those the buildings and the fields he described in his journal? Did the farmers in the fields look up to watch the noisy train pass? Did their eyes-the eyes of Popo's father, mother, brother or even Popo home on leave-look into the eyes of that German POW and wonder where he came from and where he was going? Had Franz Josef seen the small, brick church in which his grandson would be married?

Wilhelm Pingen

March 27, 1921 - January 18, 1993

Infanterie Flakregiment 44
Nachkommando

Chapter 3

Ope: A Captive's Letters

For the original project that I did for my college German course, I only compared the experiences of my grandfather Popo and Georg's grandfather Wilhelm Pingen, or Ope as Georg calls him. I decided to use Ope's experiences rather than Franz Josef's because Ope had lived much longer after the war, and I assumed that his relatives would know more about his wartime experiences.

On December 2, 1999, a week after I had interviewed Popo, I wrote an e-mail to Georg's mother and asked her what she knew about Ope's war and asked if she could find out more information. She responded with a one-page summary outlining the basic facts concerning Ope's combat and captivity. I asked more questions and received more e-mails. I compiled that information to complete my class report.

Ope was drafted in 1941 and spent three years as a soldier before his entire company was captured by British soldiers. He never saw any gruesome combat. He spent five years in a British prisoner-of-war camp in Egypt. He, like Franz Josef, did not return to Germany until January 1948, almost three years after the war had ended. Shortly after returning from captivity, he met and married Cilly Esser. They later had two children, a girl Gabriele and a boy Gert (Georg's father). He took over his family's farm near Kerpen, Germany, and lived and worked there his entire life. He grew sugar beets, wheat, potatoes, and corn and on occasion even raised a few animals.

In the latter years of his life, Ope's health declined. He found it more and more difficult to move around, and Georg's father took over the farm. As a result of Ope's deteriorating health, Georg and his younger brothers and sister never knew Ope as the fit and able farmer that he once was. However, Ope's mental health never declined, and he remained talkative until his death. His grandchildren's fondest memories of him are of sitting in the living room with him, playing cards or watching television. Ope's condition worsened from year to year until he died at age 72. Ope passed away in 1993, when Georg was 12 years old.

Ope looking out of a window of his home

Ope as a schoolboy

An overview of the buildings of the Klarahof [Ope's farm]

Wilhelm Pingen in his living room during
one of the last years of his life

Wilhelm Pingen with granddaughter Dorothee

When I went to Germany in the summer of 2000, I acquired the bulk of my information regarding Georg's family during World War II. On one occasion during that trip, I was talking to Georg's grandmother about the war when she said, "I have a lot of the letters that Ope wrote during the war. I doubt that you'll want them. They basically just say, 'Hi. How are you?'" I am sure my eyes must have lit up when she mentioned the letters, and I affirmed that I very much would like to see them. She later brought down a four-inch stack of papers bound by a rubber band. Some of the letters were torn, and they all had frayed edges. The letters were written on various forms of stationary. Some were on yellowed postcards, while others were on slick, lined paper folded together to form an envelope. There were even a few greeting cards that had been sent on special occasions.

I took the stack of letters and tried to put them in chronological order. I found that sometimes many months would pass between one letter and the next. I later learned that these were times when the prisoners were not allowed to send or receive mail during various phases of the war. I struggled to try to read each of the cards and letters. (It was my first prolonged experience with German handwriting, and I often had to ask for assistance.) I tried to figure out how the letters fit into the framework of Ope's experiences with which I was already familiar. As I read the letters, I saw amazing similarities to the letters that Popo had written; they were not full of insightful and poetic words as Franz Josef's diary had been. Many of the letters were nothing more than, "Hi. How are you? I'm fine. Hope to see you soon;" others contained questions about farm life, about family members, friends and neighbors. Others contained simple descriptions of his daily life in captivity. In fact, because Ope is no longer alive to share his memories and because he did not record his thoughts in a journal or diary, these letters are the only first-person accounts of his personal feelings and experiences during the Second World War. As I narrate Ope's story, I will include some of his letters.

Wilhelm Pingen was 20 years old when he was drafted in 1941. He had just graduated from high school and was helping run the family farm near Kerpen, Germany. His father had died when he was only nine years old, and Ope was the youngest son. His older brother Josef had already been drafted. Their mother protested against Ope's having to serve in the military, arguing that they needed him on the farm to support the family. However, her objections were to no avail.

He was first sent to Rerik, Germany, near the Baltic Sea, for his basic training. He was later sent to Sicily and then to Tripoli, Libya. Ope finally found himself in Egypt, near the Suez Canal. There his company was forced to wait for supplies before they could begin fighting. When the supplies finally arrived, they were ordered into combat. As soon as the troops marched into action, the British captured the whole company. There were no casualties.

Ope was then sent to a British prisoner-of-war camp in the Arabian Desert of Egypt. There they were forced to dig holes in the earth, which became their prison cells. In the beginning of their time in captivity, they had neither work nor food, thereby suffering from both boredom and hunger. To keep himself occupied and to earn a small income, Ope began making cigarette canisters out of pieces from destroyed bridges. He decorated them and later sold them.

From May 1944 through October 1945, Ope's family received no news from him or about him. They did not know if he was dead or alive. Ope also received no mail from home and could only imagine how his family and friends were surviving in the war-torn Germany.

The well-worn cover of Wilhelm Pingen's soldierbook

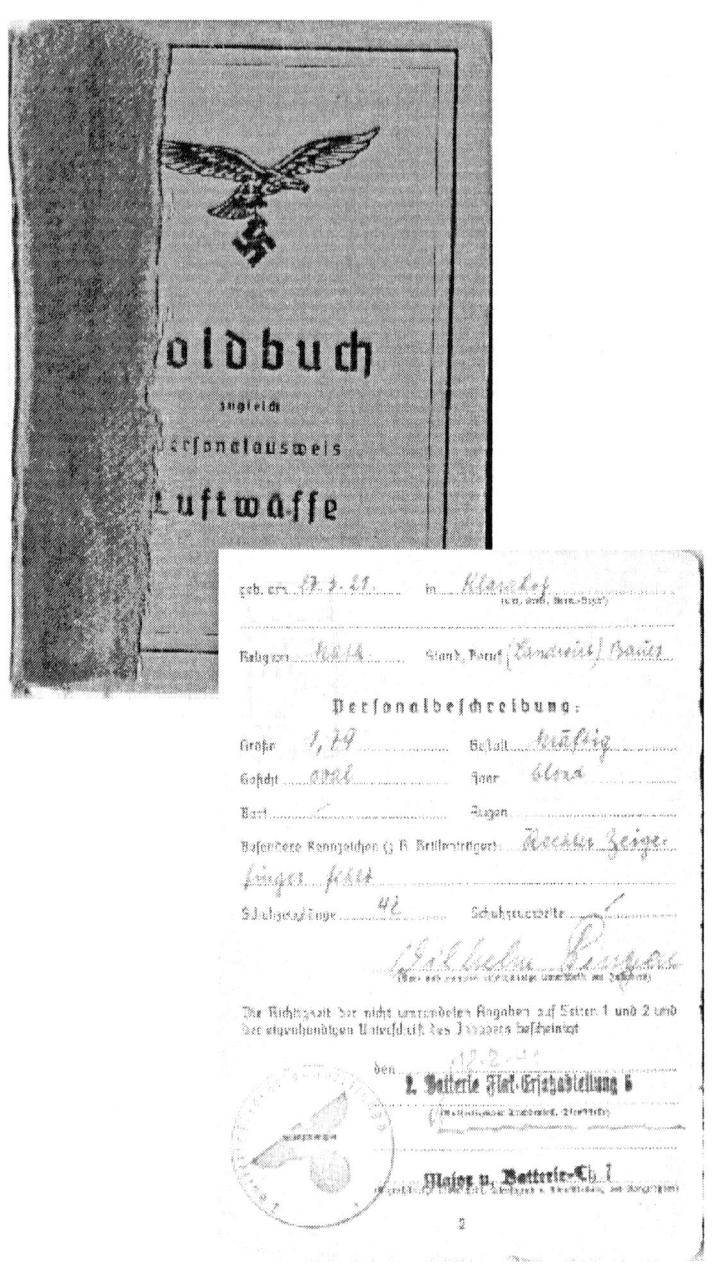

A page of Ope's soldierbook that lists personal characteristics, including the fact that he was missing his right index finger

P.

Anfangsbuchstabe
des Familiennamens
des Absenders

I. TEIL

EIN MITGLIED DER GESCHLAGENEN
WEHRMACHT SUCHT SEINEN
NÄCHSTEN ANGEHÖRIGEN

Ich bin noch am Leben und befinde mich z. Z. in ~~amerikanischer~~ britischer ~~russischer~~ Hand

Ich bin gesund ~~im Lazarett~~   Meine Anschrift ist wie unten.   Bitte die Karte sofort zurückzuschicken !

Datum 2. Januar 1946   Unterschrift Willi Pingen

Geburtsort und Geburtsdatum Blatzheim 27.0.21

II. TEIL.

Briefmarke

Zulässige Anschrift des Wehrmachtsangehörigen
IN BLOCKSCHRIFT

Diensgrad, Name, Vorname: Obergefreiter Willi Pingen
382 P W Camp N80989
P.W. Postal Section
Middle-East-Egypt

The letter that the Pingen family received informing them of Ope's status as a POW. The letter reads: A member of the defeated German armed forces is looking for his next-of-kin. I am still alive and find myself in British hands. I am healthy. My address is as follows. Please send this card directly back. Date: Jaunary 2, 1946

In October Ope's family finally heard from someone in a nearby town that Ope was alive but had been taken prisoner. Three months later they received this news officially and learned that he was healthy. In February they received their first letter from him. This, however, did not end the communication problems, and there were several other periods when the family and Ope lived for several months with no news from each other. The following letter was among the first that Ope was able to send home:

Dear Mother! Dear Siblings! May 22, 1946

Thank you very much for your loving letter from April 3. I am happy that you are all still doing well and that everything is as it always was. I hope that you're getting mail from me. I could not write from the end of the war until the beginning of February. After that, I wrote 2 letters and 4 cards in March. And don't worry about me, I am fine. Now I am in a workhouse; the food situation here is good. You asked, dear Magda, if we had heard anything regarding our release. We only hear rumors about that, nothing exact. We can only patiently wait and hope that the day of freedom is not far off. That will be some reunion. What do you mean that I unnecessarily torment myself about your worrying about me? From what I gathered from your letter, you, dear Josef, are able to help out again with your arm without any problems. Everything is working out with the business. I wondered if you could get enough fuel for the tractor. How many people do you have now and what kinds of people? How is the cow stall coming along? Do you have fewer cattle now? I hope that I can soon be with you all. I continue in that hope. With my best regards and wishes, especially to you, dear Mother. Your grateful Willi

After the war had ended, the prisoners received points based on factors such as marital status and number of children in order to determine which prisoners would be sent home first. Just like Popo, Ope had few points and was forced to remain in the POW camp.

The year 1946 was an especially difficult year for Ope and his family because his mother became deathly ill. Ope's mother and sisters did not want to add to Ope's burdens while he was in prison and thus did not tell him of his mother's illness. When Mrs. Pingen died in the summer of 1946, his sisters still did not tell him the news. Ope continued sending letters to his mother for several months before his sisters decided that they had to tell him. Below is one of the letters he wrote to his mother after she had already passed away:

My dear Mother! Dear Siblings! Sunday, July 7, 1946

Thank you again for your loving letter from May 2. I am happy to learn that at this point everything is still just like always. Especially to you, dear Mother and to you, dear sisters, I send my best wishes for your upcoming Saints' Days. We hope that this will be the last Saint's Day when I cannot orally extend my best wishes to you. I am doing fine, as well. I have enough to eat, and my health is the same as always. Today I went swimming with Fritz Portz in the Mediterranean Sea. We had to be chained up on the way there, but we already have a lot more freedom than before. You would just like to be able to take a little walk in the woods, but unfortunately there isn't anything like that here. Right now the sun here is really nice again; well, we've gotten used to it. A lot of comrades here are receiving mail telling how bad everything in the cities is, and even in the towns. Hopefully, that will all be over after the harvest. From my experience between October '45 and April '46, I already know what it feels like to be hungry. Therefore, I can imagine that many people are using dishonest means to get food. The prices are also not very low right now. By the way, what is Gelda up to? I haven't heard anything from her. I leave you with my loving regards, to you, dear Mother, to you dear siblings, and to you Franz W. Your grateful Willi

After he had learned of his mother's death and had learned that his sisters had tried to shield him from the news, Wilhelm wrote the following letter to his younger brother, Josef:

September 22, 1946

My dear Josef! I thank you so much for your loving letter from August 13. I am happy that until now you and everyone else are doing so well, and I hope that these words find you in the best of health. Everything is the same as always here and except for my lack of freedom, I am doing very well. Hopefully I can be with all of you soon. I can tell you and promise you that we will always get along well with one another, and we will have a lot to catch up on. If our good, dear Mother could only experience it with us! From here I still cannot imagine that I will find an empty bed and room. Yes, dear Josef, in captivity you become indifferent. They younger prisoners have many illusions about being discharged and are always disappointed. They can't do that to us anymore. One day, the day of freedom will suddenly be there, whether it be soon or a long way off. I have one request of you, dear Brother, please write me about everything that is going on at home. Don't keep anything a secret from me. I am very happy that Magda [his sister] and Franz [her boyfriend] are getting along well with one another. You know that I have always thought a lot of him. I haven't heard anything from the relatives. I received a simple card from Heinrich. I tell you this, they had better not bother me about it later. I am glad that everything is going well on the Klarahof [the farm]. In the hope that I am with you all again soon, I send you and everyone else many very loving regards and wishes. Your dear brother, Willi

Letter Ope sent to his mother on July 7, 1946

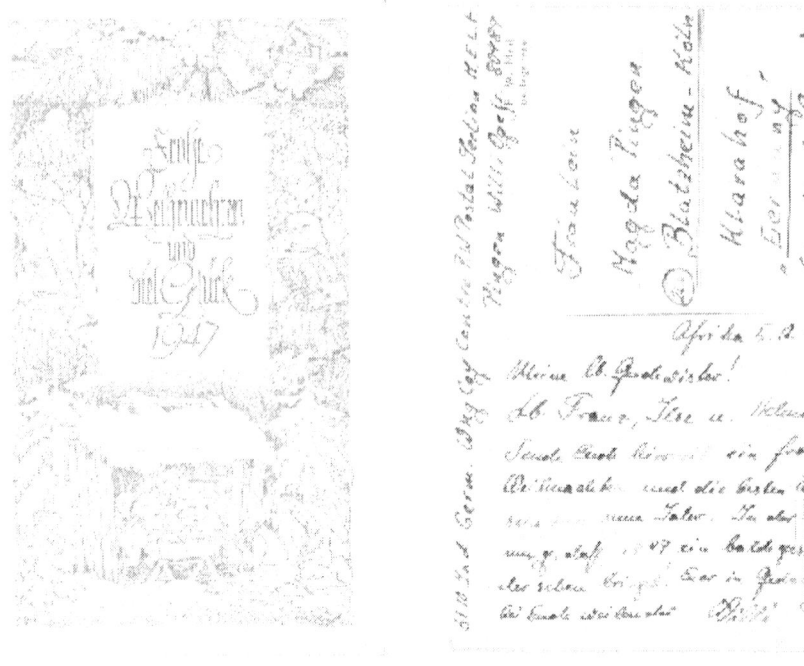

The front and back of a Christmas card that Ope sent in 1946. The front reads: *Merry Christmas and a lot of luck in 1947.* The back reads: *My dear Siblings, dear Franz, Else and Helvis! With this I send you a merry Christmas and best wishes for the New Year. In the hope that 1947 brings a swift reunion! Staying with you in your thoughts, Willi*

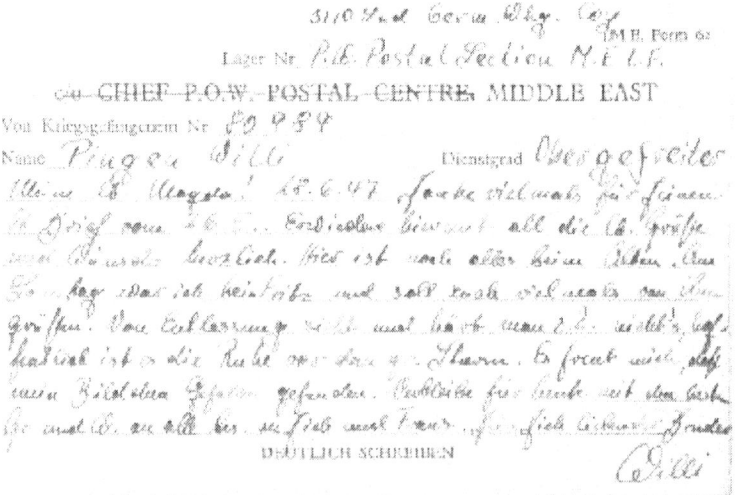

A postcard Ope sent to his sister Magda on June 18, 1947

In 1947 Ope wrote many letters, all of course anxiously awaiting his release. The prisoners were treated much better than they had been in the beginning, and often it was easy to forget that he was a prisoner while reading the letters. One such letter follows:

My dear Siblings! Dear Franz and children! Easter '47.

I send you all my most sincere Easter greetings and hope that you had a great day. As far as I'm concerned, I can't complain. The days were filled with welcome changes from the daily routine; we had from Good Friday to the next Monday off. We built us a paddleboat and had a great time paddling on the Beaver Sea and in the Suez Canal; it was wonderful. Among other things, I learned a new sport; we went fishing. Yes, dear Franz, that would be a little substitute for hunting. You really have to talk fancy, so that these little beasts will bite. Yes, as I'm sure you all can imagine, we were busy the whole day from 5 in the morning until 10 at night. In the evenings we went to the movies. Of course, it would have been better if we could have seen some German films. The food was good and plenty. Today at noon Lebens [a friend] came to visit me. Unfortunately he lives a long ways away and couldn't stay long. There isn't any real progress concerning our release. Right now some of the vehicles aren't running again; of course that affects when we'll be released. But don't worry about me. The day can't be far off; then your man will be with you again. As you can see, we are not living badly here right now. There is a very fertile region around our camp. Here they are already harvesting the wheat and the barley. Eight days ago I took a little stroll through the countryside. This coming Sunday, I'm going to visit Fritz Portz, wanted to go last Sunday, but didn't make it. All the vehicles were out in the fields. My regards to Klein. How is it going with your things in Sindorf, dear Magda; hopefully I'll receive some good news from this relationship soon. For today, my loving regards and wishes, also to Horst. Your "loving-you" Willi

Most of the letters from 1947 were all very similar to one another. They were postcards and were thus short and only contained basic information. One such letter, addressed to his sister Magda follows:

My dear Magda! June 18, 1947

Thank you very much for your loving letter from May 26. With this letter I return all of the loving regards and wishes. Everything is still the same here. On Sunday I was with Fritz and am supposed to greet you from him. Right now we are not seeing or hearing anything regarding our release; hopefully it's the calm before the big storm. I am happy that you like my little pictures. For today, I leave you and everyone with my regards and best wishes, especially to you and Franz. Your "loving-you" Brother Willi

A few of the letters from 1947 were longer and contained more detailed information about the camp and about how Ope kept himself occupied. One such letter follows. This was the last letter in the stack and possibly the last letter that Ope wrote as a prisoner-of-war.

Dear Siblings! Dear Franz! August 13, 1947

Thank you very much for your loving letter from July 16, dear Magda. Likewise, I thank you very much, dear Greta, for your engagement announcement. I am happy that you have this day comfortably and joyfully behind you. Today one month has already gone by, and I am still sitting here in this same old place. I gather from that that it will all work out soon. I cannot say exactly when because we live in constant uncertainty. Otherwise, everything is the same as always here. Health wise I'm doing very well. I'm happy that you also concluded that from my photos. I can't complain about the food. The heat has already lightened up a bit. For a while, it wasn't nice anymore; every time you shook someone's hand, you would break out into a sweat. During the last few days after a long struggle, I was able to get a meter of formal linen; it's enough for a suit. If the finance department will allow me to, I will buy me something else. I've been planning to buy one meter of camel's hair; it's the same as horsehair back home. You will already have the harvest behind you. Because it's so dry, you won't have the best yield. One just about has to conclude that everything is cursed against us Germans. And on top of all that, the potato beetle plague; it's almost too much of a good thing. I am happy that the third colt was delivered in good condition and that it's a good animal. I am already very much looking forward to the cherry preserves. Right now, things like that seem foreign. So I will happily eat up all the preserves, and then I don't need to pick out the pits anymore, another advantage. On Sunday I'm going to Fritz' and am supposed to tell you hello from him. My loving regards to the little one and to Horst. Hopefully I can soon help him. The poor guy has also had to endure a lot. In the hope of hearing from you again soon, I continue in the best regards and wishes. In the hope of a swift reunion, dear Siblings, Franz, Else and Helen. Your grateful Willi

The entrance to the camp where Ope was a POW for 5 years

Ope (third left,backrow) stands with
some of the other POW's in Egypt

Photos Ope took of the Egyptian countryside

Ope finally returned home to the Klarahof, his farm near Sindorf, Germany, in the beginning of 1948. He had not seen his family in eight years.

As I read Ope's letters, it did not seem that he had suffered to the extent that either Popo or Franz Josef had. He had not seen his friends and fellow soldiers die in battle, nor did his letters express the longing and loneliness that Franz Josef's journal did. In fact, in many of the letters and photographs he seemed to be a tourist rather than a prisoner-of-war. His letters talked of racing paddleboats in the Suez Canal, going to the movies, and visiting friends.

But what had not been recorded in those letters? In the beginning of his captivity, he had not been allowed to write. Those were supposedly the worst days, the days when they had been without food or work. What had happened then? I thought about what Popo had said, describing a POW camp from the perspective of a captor, *"When they walked into the hospital room* [of the POW camp], *that patient had to stand up and stand at attention. If they just had one leg, they still had to prop up. It was rough on them. Our troops were mean, too, some of them. But we were taught to be mean, just like Georg's granddaddies were taught. Of course, we was all young and didn't care either."*

After enduring the months of unwritten hardships, Ope learned that his mother, whom he had obviously loved dearly, had died. He was in Egypt alone. He could not attend her funeral or be there to comfort his sisters. In fact, he did not even find out about her death until months after she had passed away. He lived a year in captivity hoping for his release but knowing that home would not be the same, knowing that his mother would not be there for the reunion. He had alluded to his pain in his letter to his brother Josef but had not even mentioned his mother's death in any of the other letters. Ope's letters were different from Franz Josef's diary in that Ope knew that someone would read what he wrote. He knew that his family had enough troubles of their own and did not want them to worry about him. Did he therefore not write about all of his pain and troubles? His sisters had not told him about his mother's illness and death to save him the burden. What had he not told them?

I thought about Ope's war in comparison with the wars that Popo and Franz Josef had faced. Like Popo, Ope had been drafted off of his family's farm when he was only 19 years old. Like Franz Josef, he had been taken prisoner not long after going into battle. He had suffered the same fears and disappointments that Franz Josef had concerning his family and his release. Because I can no longer ask Ope about his experiences, I am left with many of the same questions that I have about Franz Josef. What was it like when he returned home? Did his brother and sisters recognize him after he had been gone for eight years? Did he have to deal with his mother's death all over again? Did he ever talk about the war?

James W. Davis
Born: April 29, 1926

Chapter 4

Pa: A Farmer's Story

After I had compiled all of the interviews, letters, documents, photographs, and the diary for our three veteran grandfathers, I realized that I had not talked to my other grandfather, whom I call Pa. Pa also lives in Gadsden, Tennessee. He is married and has two children (one of whom is my mother) and four grandchildren. I knew that Pa had not been in the military during the war and therefore originally decided that his story would not be consistent with my research. I then began to examine his situation more carefully. He was the same age as Popo, yet he had not been drafted. According to Popo, almost all of the young men his age had been drafted unless they had rich or powerful connections or unless they were physically unable.

I thought about what I knew about Pa's background. He was from Gadsden, Tennessee. His parents (my great grandparents) lived in a small square wooden house situated on less than an acre of land. The white paint was peeling off of the outside. In fact, it was probably very similar to the "halfway fallen-in, dirty huts" that Franz Josef had described so vividly in his diary. I knew that the family also owned a few acres of farming land but definitely nothing of great value. It was difficult for me to imagine that Pa had ever had any rich or powerful friends or relatives that could have interfered with his being drafted.

I then considered the second possibility. Was he physically unable to be a soldier? He had been having trouble with his knees during the past few years, but that seemed to be a recent problem rather than an injury from his youth. As long as I had known him, he had always been fairly active. Before he had retired, he had owned a small grocery store and gas station and thus knew everything that was going on in Gadsden. He has a barn behind his house, where he spends much of his time. There he keeps cows, mules, chickens, guineas, dogs, and any other animals that happen to find their way to the barn. He is proud of his covered wagon, and on special occasions he hitches his mules up to it and drives it around town. He also loves to hunt and fish. Taking all of this into consideration, it was difficult for me to imagine that he would have any physical handicap that would not have permitted him to serve in the military.

Finally, out of curiosity I decided to interview him. Unlike with Popo, I did not have to wonder what my first question would be. I knew exactly how to begin the interview, and so I asked him, "Why did you not have to serve in the war?"

In his small-town, Southern drawl, he answered very matter-of-factly, "They claimed I had one leg shorter 'n the other. I was put on active duty but no marchin'. And then, that's all I ever knew. They never did call me up." As he answered, his face showed no sign of relief or regret or any feelings whatsoever about not being drafted. That was just the way it had happened, and he had accepted that. He concluded his statement as though that was all he had to say about the whole war and about his whole experience during the war.

I had to ask him many questions in order to piece his story together because I often only received one-word or one-sentence answers. I learned that he was eighteen years old and had been going to school and farming when he had been ordered to report to the draft board. "I'd work at home all the week and pull the plough all day on Saturday for the neighbors for fifty cents. That's what I'd get, fifty cents, and was glad to get it." He had also been attending school but dropped out for a year after the eleventh grade.

I stayed out of school the last year. They told me down at Alamo, there wasn't no use in me startin'. I would have to go [to the war], and then it come up, and I never did have to go, and I got up and went back to school the next day. Mother come in there and woke me up and said, "Get up and go to school." And I got up and went to school.

I also found out that Pa had been ordered to report to the military twice. He first went for his physical examination. Later he was ordered to report to Fort Oglethorpe, Georgia in 1943. As was the case with many of the soldiers, the trip to basic training was the farthest from home he had ever been.

I thought I was gone for good that time. When I went to Georgia is when they said I had one leg a little shorter than the other. That's when they said that I never would have to go out on the field to do no marchin'. Well, see, I kept thinkin' they was goin' to call me back up. They said if it come up, you know, that they needed somethin' that I could do without my legs being a problem, they'd call me back. Never did do it, I don't reckon.

I asked him if he had previously known that his legs were not the same length. He replied, "I knew that I always had to

Pa at Christmas, 1997

Pa at his barn with his covered wagon and chickens

cut one britches leg off a little shorter, if I got a nice pair of pants. It wouldn't hang right." He was serious, but I had to laugh at his response.

Finally, I asked him how the war had affected his life. He thought about it a moment and then said with a shrug, "Well, I never did know too much about it. I spent three weeks up at Fort Oglethorpe, Georgia, the last time before they...I could tell you a pretty good size tale on that." After convincing him that I wanted to hear the story, he continued:

Well, they carried me up and marched me down this long hall everyday for a week or longer. I stayed there about three weeks. They called out on the loud speaker that I need to report up there to Building, I forgot what number it was. And they told me they was fixin' to send me home. I didn't know 'til then what they were gonna do with me. So this boy that was in there fillin' out the papers; he was crippled. He says I don't see no way I can get you outta here to the train station until in the mornin'. He fooled around there a little longer and he says, "Let me go down here just a minute." And he come back in a jeep. He says, "I can carry you to the station tonight." And I still had my meal tickets; I never did eat a bite comin' home. They give me some meal tickets to come back home.

That was the end of Pa's war story. I was amazed at how sheltered he had been from the war. I asked him if he remembered where he had been when Pearl Harbor was bombed. He said, "I remember it, but I couldn't tell you where I was." "What about when the war ended?" I asked. "I still couldn't tell you. That's been a long time ago." I asked him if he remembered what his feelings toward the Germans were during the war or how they had been portrayed in the media. He simply replied, "I never had no dealin's with 'em." "Were any members of your immediate family sent overseas? Did you write to any of the soldiers?" He shook his head.

The more questions I asked, the more astonished I became. How was this possible? I had just researched three men whose lives had been absolutely consumed by the war, and I was sitting here talking to a man who was the same age as they, who had lived through the same historical era as they, who was even from the same small town as one of them, and yet, with the exception of three weeks of his life spent in training camp, he had managed to remain virtually unscathed by the war.

I have read a number of books about the Second World War, as well as many personal accounts of the war, but I had never read of anyone who had lived through that time period either on the front lines or on the home front without the war having had a dramatic impact on his or her life. I had never thought about people just continuing living their daily lives; in all of the books that I had read, it seemed as though the whole world had stopped when the war had started. As Pa described his experiences of working, going to school, and dating, I suddenly realized that there were many lives that still went on as usual despite the major war. The cows still had to be milked, the fields still had to be ploughed, the children still had to go to school.

I thought about the lives of Popo, Franz Josef, and Ope. Their young lives had been put on hold for several years because of the war, and when they returned they were not the same men who had left. The war had turned their lives upside down. For them the war was a violent tempest that had ripped apart their homes and their lives. However, Pa taught me that, at least in America, there were others. There were those who had remained at home, those who had continued going to school and continued chopping cotton. To them, the war was

Pa as a young man

Pa on his tractor after the war

Pa's ration book

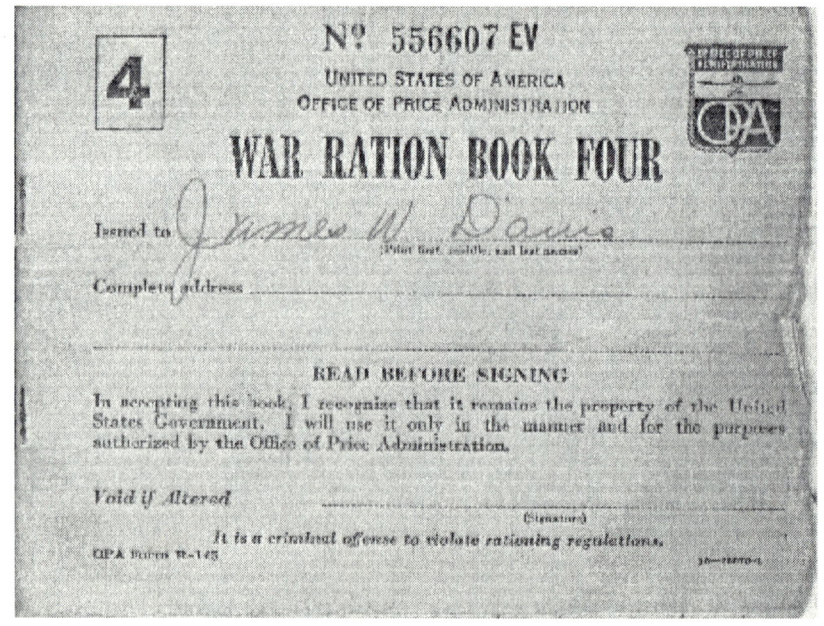

Pa's ration book holder

Part II

Our Grandmothers

Cilly Esser Pingen
Born: May 23, 1929

Chapter 5

Onnu: A Child's Reflection

What all have you lived through and what is still in front of you—you brides, wives, and mothers? The homeland in danger, the men on the front, or like me, in captivity and without news-uncertainty, fear, and worry.

That is the manner in which Franz Josef described the women on the home front when he recorded his thoughts in his diary in September of 1944. When I initially began my project, I only planned to investigate the experiences of the soldiers, our grandfathers. I had not considered how much the women at home had also been affected by the war. After reading Franz Josef's thoughts I began to think about these women, our grandmothers, and what they too must have endured. And as the project further developed, I kept finding myself talking more and more to our grandmothers. When I first interviewed Popo, my grandmother kept interjecting information that Popo neglected to tell me, and she was the one who made sure that I had all of the photographs, documents, and books that I could possibly use in my research. When I interviewed Pa, it was again my grandmother who continually reminded him of events that he had forgotten and encouraged him to say everything that he could remember about his experiences. And then when I began to uncover the stories of Georg's grandfathers, I was almost completely reliant on his grandmothers for the information. They were the ones who knew their husbands' stories best. It was they who had the diary, the letters, and the photographs; they were the ones who helped me piece their husbands' war experiences together.

As I carried out my research, I began to hear bits and pieces of our grandmothers' own stories. As they told the husbands' stories or as they listened to their husbands tell them, they would occasionally offer details about their own experiences on the German and American home fronts. All four of our grandmothers were several years younger than their husbands. Franz Josef's wife, Omi, had been 13 when the war had started, and the other three were only children. For this reason, I decided that I wanted to hear these women's experiences; they would offer me the opportunity to not only see the war from the perspective of women on the home front but it would also allow me to see the war through the eyes of children, children that were too young to understand the worldwide political objectives of the war, children that could only understand how the war affected their own young lives in their own little corner of the world.

When I went to Germany in the summer of 2000, one of the first things I wanted to do was to ask Georg's grandmother, whom her grandchildren call Onnu, about her experiences in the war. When I thought about it, the same fear I had felt when I was planning to interview Popo crept back into my mind, only with Popo I had been talking to my own grandfather in my own country. And Popo had been one of the "good guys," one of the victors. Now I was stepping into someone else's family, someone else's country, a country that had lost the war and a country whose citizens had suffered much shame because of their deeds during the war. I was afraid as I imagined some of the possible outcomes of the interview. Would she have been too young to remember it? Would she refuse to talk about? Or, worst of all, would she feel personally offended, as though I were accusing her of being a Nazi simply by my asking about the war?

Onnu lives with Georg's family on the Klarahof, the family's farm, and I felt that I had gotten to know her fairly well during my prior two visits to Germany. She did most of the cooking for the family (and is a very good cook, I might add), and at night we would usually go to her part of the house to watch television or to play card games. I always think of her as being the typical German in the way she scrutinizes everyone and everything she sees on television. She is also a typical grandmother and spoils her six grandchildren (in a good way, of course). She always makes time to play games with Georg's youngest brother or to drive his older siblings to any of the places they need to go. She always makes sure that everything is done the way it is supposed to be done. She bakes beautiful cakes, grows lovely flowers, and is an excellent hostess.

But as I approached her to interview her, I was scared. I decided that rather than just beginning the interview, I would first just ask her if it would be okay for me to talk to her sometime about what she had experienced during World War II. That would give her the opportunity to decline if she did not want to talk about it for any reason. One night at the Klarahof, Georg and I were coming down the stairs when we met Onnu coming out of the kitchen. With a little nudging from my fiancé, I politely and reservedly asked her if I could carry out the interview. She seemed slightly surprised by my request but then nodded her head in agreement. Then, after a little thought, she began, "Yeah, we were the first civilians that they had encountered, the Allies when they came through here. West of here they'd all been evacuated, but they didn't evacuate us." She then continued and told me several stories about sleeping on the floor of a church and about encountering a black soldier after the war. After she had talked for half an hour, I stopped her because I wanted to have the stories on a tape recorder and did not want to have to ask her to repeat herself. After that, I realized that I probably would not have any trouble getting these German women to talk about their wartime experiences, and I was correct. They seemed to have hours' worth of stories stored up in their minds and were just waiting to have the opportunity to share them.

The day after I had asked Onnu if I could interview her, she, Georg, and I sat down at the dining room table, and she began to talk. We did not need to ask many questions; for the most part, she just told her story from the beginning to the end.

Before the war I was still too young to understand the seriousness of what was going on. I was ten years old when the war began. We were actually hoping that the war would start, so that something exciting would be going on. The war would be interesting. The first two years were quiet, until the first air raids began. I was in school then.

Onnu was living with her mother, her older sister, and her grandfather on a farm called Breitmaar. The farm is right outside of Sindorf, Germany and is not far from Georg's family's farm, the Klarahof. Breitmaar is actually a 500-year-old castle, and Onnu's sister Annemie and Annemie's son Axel still live there. When the war started, Onnu was attending a boarding school in Düren, a town about ten miles from her home.

In Düren the situation kept getting more serious. There were air-raid sirens day and night. The Allies dropped leaflets that said, "Düren in the hole, we'll find you anyways." This relatively small city was important to them because there was a hydroelectric power plant nearby that provided the water for the city and for the people in the surrounding area. Besides that, the low-lying city would have been flooded. They didn't succeed. The English and the Americans also bombed the railroads: Paris, Brussels, Aachen, Düren, Cologne until Berlin. It was used by the politicians and the military.

We spent most of our time at the school in the cellar. Classes were held there and we did our work on our wooden beds. Everyone copied off of each other; that was the only good thing. Otherwise, we were scared to death. In October of 1944 the school was closed because it was too dangerous. We only had a few hours to pack up our things and go home. Two days later the school and the dorms were leveled. The nuns and some of the teachers were killed. They were supposed to leave the school a week later, but of course then it was too late. Düren was 80% destroyed. After the school was closed, I went back to Breitmaar. Even in Breitmaar the windows were shattered because of the bombing in Düren.

Georg then broke in with a question that I had wanted to ask but was afraid to. He said, "How much did you have to do with the Hitler Youth?"

When you are in a boarding school, you look for every opportunity to get out. There is not getting away from Catholic nuns. They suffered a lot under the Nazis. They weren't allowed to teach at all anymore; they were only allowed to manage the boarding school. They were forced to send us to Hitler Youth meetings two nights a week: one hour of exercise, one hour of singing. We had fun, but that didn't influence me very much, I honestly have to say.

Onnu (front) with older sister before the beginning of the war

Onnu (right) with sister Annemie

She seemed to be finished, so I tried to think of other questions. "How many siblings did you have?" I asked her.

One sister. After I was back in Breitmaar with my mother, grandfather, and sister-our help had also moved in with our family-I received an order from our regional director, who was a Nazi, to go and dig trenches. My mother tried to get me an exemption, but it didn't help and was denied. So I, along with other teenagers (15 year olds), were put on trucks and taken to Horrem. They gave us shovels and under military observation, we began working. That hopeless undertaking only lasted two days because some reconnaissance planes had found us, and some low-flying aircraft shot at us. So we were taken further, in order to cook for an anti-aircraft unit, where the so-called Flakhelfer [anti-aircraft gun assistants] were. They were one year older than us, 16 years old. This position was also discovered and fired at. They couldn't hold the position. The boys were sent to northern Germany, and finally went home. The young Flakhelfer were all crying when they left. They were scared and homesick.

In the meantime the cellar in Breitmaar had been furnished. Comfortable chairs, that you could also sleep in, a couch for my sister, who was pregnant. Her husband was an officer in the air force during the war. Each one of us was assigned a sack to take with us in case we had to flee: jewelry, papers, silver, work papers, etc. Now we were hoping that the Allies would liberate us and bring about the end of this terrible war. But because Hitler's insanity drove the soldiers and the people to ruin, it kept going on and on. Because our cellar had very thick walls, we felt somewhat safe, at least until February 15. Both the German and Americans threw grenades at Breitmaar; it was as though they were taking a fortress. One grenade hit the hatch to the cellar. A cloud of dust came into the rooms of the cellar. We had cut away some stones in a thinner wall for a possible escape route. We had to get out that way and ran up a second stairway to get outside and to the pasture in front of the house. One of the men that worked for us advised us to lie down in the grenade and bomb craters. He claimed, "A second shot rarely hits the same hole." That worked. He was an experienced solder from the First World War, where he had lost one of his legs. The shrapnel whistled over us. One time when we were in one of the bomb craters, a grenade came, and my mother ducked her head really quickly. She hit her head on someone else's foot, but didn't know for a long time if she had been hit by the grenade or not.

The stalls were burning and the cattle and horses were pathetically mooing and neighing. After everything had calmed down a little bit, we went back to take care of our grandfather, who absolutely did not want to leave the house. He put his index finger in the air and said, "This is the end." The men drove the cows, horses, and pigs out of the stalls. The animals were panicking and kept trying to get back in the stalls. Many of the animals had already been shot because of serious burns. The Americans had taken over Breitmaar, but they kept right on shooting. The Germans were still here, if they just had one more bullet or one more bomb. We always listened to the enemy station on the radio, which could have almost meant the death penalty. We weren't ever allowed to listen to enemy stations. We saw what was taking place, though, and always believed the enemy station more than the German one.

Georg asked her, "Were you glad that the Americans came?" Onnu answered with an emphatic, "Yes!"

That was indeed a liberation. First of all, none of us were Nazis, my father especially not. He died in 1943; he'd had trouble with his heart for a long time. He was 48. And in the middle of 1944 he got a draft notice; that was really morbid. Even if it were children, every person had to do his part. We didn't have any more people then. And the "Volkssturm"-those were the people that were here-the old men, they had to protect the civilians. For example, they always had to walk back and forth between Breitmaar and Sindorf.

While we were in the cellar, an American soldier suddenly appeared. He was a black man. He was drunk, had taken over our wine cellar. He put us-all 14 of us-on the wall, and he wanted to shoot us. We tried to explained to him that we were civilians and were happy about the liberation, but he just kept getting angrier and angrier. He wasn't all there anymore, but we didn't know that. We just thought they were like that, so wild and violent and mean, and they planned to shoot us. Of course we were crying. Then an officer came-I suppose it was his boss-and took his gun away from him. He calmed us down and promised us that nothing was going to happen to us. They weren't going to shoot civilians. I think that he was relieved himself that he could stop something bad from happening at the last moment, when we thought that it was all over.

Then the Americans came and reported what they were going to do with us. We were the first civilians that they had encountered. All of the towns and farms before us had been evacuated. They were clueless. So they sent us to the neighboring farm, the Klarahof-that's been my home now for more than 50 years-with our hands in the air. And woe to the person who took his hands down just a little bit; then they would come and put their gun directly in your back and say, "Raise your hands higher." We spent most of the time lying on the ground because of the bombing. Ope's mother and sister gave us money, clothes, and something to eat. We weren't allowed to stay there. My sister and my grandfather were put in a military vehicle and were taken to the next stop. My grandfather, who was a little confused, insulted the Americans. After his stroke, he wasn't able to understand everything anymore. He always wanted to have his say. I tried to use my schoolgirl English to explain to the Americans that he didn't mean it. They calmed me down and gave my grandfather

Refugee family from the far western part of Germany that stayed at Breitmaar

The main house at Breitmaar with the animals in the yard

and me chocolate and cookies. He couldn't bite them anymore, but that didn't matter. So they were very, very kind to those who needed help, except for that one black drunk.

Then we were put on trucks and taken to the church in Golsheim. My sister got a bed in the priests' quarter. The rest of us had to sleep on straw piles on the floor. My sister always got good food and coffee. Sometimes that made me very jealous. If you had to go to the bathroom, even then a soldier had to go with you. He stood in front of you, turned around because there were no doors. He didn't look, but we were of course scared. After two sleepless nights, we went on to Düren. Ironically our destination was called Paradise Place. We were put into a small room there with 15 people. We had to sleep on the floor, and every time one person turned over, everyone had to turn over. Of course, we were fed up with all of this, and there was some friction.

We went into the cellar of the house, which we really weren't allowed to do. Everything was destroyed there, everything open. We didn't have anything to eat, absolutely nothing. We survived ten days on some canned green beans that we had found in the cellar of the house. And the Americans had given us some bread. So, what did we eat? Bread and beans, beans and bread. Only Annemie, she was well taken care of. She got peanut butter, a lot of white bread (this American bread), and ground coffee, and my mother always had her eye on that ground coffee.

In Golsheim we had to get on trucks and were told that we would be taken to France, Belgium, or Holland, in order to help with the reconstruction. Our truck was destined to go to Belgium, and we were all counted and put on the truck. Our grandfather wasn't taken with us. They took him back to Breitmaar, where he died all alone. The thought of that was terrible for us. He was buried together with dead soldiers. When we came back, we had him reburied in the family grave.

Breitmaar. Thye bridge was destroyed during the war and was never rebuilt.

Onnu's grandfather going hunting. He is on the far right side with his index finger in the air. Hi is still giving orders, just like Onnu described him.

We then stopped in Düren, and they told us that we would continue driving to Belgium later. But that never happened. They must have seen that we wouldn't have been much help with construction.

When we came back home, we found out that Breitmaar had been completely destroyed. I don't know if they hadn't found the heating fuel or that was just too much trouble for them, but they had chopped up all of the furniture in Breitmaar with an ax in order to build a fire. The whole house was furnished, and then there was nothing left. At that time we had real carpets; they were huge in Breitmaar. But they had cut all of the Persian rugs into 4-cornered pieces and had hung them over the windows to keep it nice and warm because there wasn't glass in them anymore.

We begin to clean up in Breitmaar. We couldn't even think about living there. Some acquaintances let us have two bedrooms in Sindorf. So every morning we walked to Breitmaar and then in the evening walked back. On March 17, my sister began having labor pains. My uncle, who was a doctor, came to her, and she had a son, Axel, that we put in a borrowed cradle in our room. He was born three weeks early and was very little. After he was three weeks old and was healthy, because we had a really nice, warm spring, my friend and I took him to Breitmaar in a baby carriage. There I saw a black soldier standing by the baby carriage. My friend immediately hid in a closet, but I couldn't leave Axel alone. We were so scared of the blacks because of that earlier experience with the drunk soldier and because we hadn't seen many black people before. And then one of the black soldiers came over to Axel and began to play with him. Of course, I was scared out of my mind for Axel and then went over there and made it clear to the black man with my little bit of English that he should leave Axel alone. Then the soldier pulled out his wallet and showed me a picture of his baby, that was about the same age as Axel. That was such a nice man, and how he got out the picture.

A few weeks later a jeep came to our farm. The officer and his driver asked us about dead soldiers that may have been buried in the pastures or fields because they were in a hurry. I went with them and showed them what I thought were graves. When he saw the little hills, he had to laugh and said, "Those aren't graves. They're latrines." I hadn't seen any before, and that was a little embarrassing for me.

Although the war wasn't over for the whole country, our future already looked brighter. We could live in Breitmaar again before winter. It wasn't possible to buy anything yet. Only doing business on the black market, but others did that for us. The Americans lived in surplus, and anything they threw out at the railway embankment, we went and got. So we weren't in need; most of all we had learned to be inventive in the last few years. Eight o'clock at night was curfew; after that no one was allowed on the streets. I don't know exactly when all of these limitations were abolished. After years of fear, we felt free and happy. I think that a person can only experience this feeling after living through such an era.

After the war it took a long time before the schools were opened again. One of the first schools was the nun school in Düren. Of course, I went back there, so that I would get my diploma. I got my diploma in spring 1946 and got my "mittlere Reife." [There are varying degrees of high school diplomas in Germany depending on the school a person attends; this was the middle diploma]. *But that was a joke because the first year after the war the school didn't have any stringent requirements.*

Onnu seemed to be finished with her wartime experiences, so I decided to ask one final question that would allow me to join Onnu's and Ope's stories. "When and how did you and Ope meet?" I asked.

In 1949. He just came back from captivity in '48. It was pretty soon after he came back. I first met him in Cologne at a horse-riding tournament; he had just been back two or three weeks. He had a good body, not like those from Russia, that needed a half of a year to even look human again. He really looked good, was tanned brown and also strong; he didn't really have to make up for anything. At the tournament in Cologne, we just greeted each other, and then a week later he came to Breitmaar on the tractor and said "Hello" to my mother. Maybe as I look back, I already knew something must be up because before that they had never really spoken to one another. I don't even know if my mother knew who it was. Then there was a fire on the Klarahof. The field barn burned down; someone had set it on fire. And then I went with Axel's grandfather to go look at it. Then we went to a riding tournament in Bedburg, and then Ope came and asked me if we would mind taking his uncle home because they still wanted to go to the riding ball. Then I thought, "That's rude. Instead of asking me if I want to go with him to the riding ball, he brings his uncle into it." Then I told him that our carriage was full. That wasn't true, but I was so mad. And then Ope's brother called and asked if I could get him tickets for the riding ball in Bergerhausen. And that was very difficult; only certain people could get tickets and then I got the tickets, but didn't know who all would come along. There along with some others, was Ope. Yes, and then we really got to know one another.

They did indeed get to know one another, and one year later Onnu and Ope were married. They lived on the Klarahof and had two children and six grandchildren. Onnu has lived her life as a homemaker, helping take care of her family and the farm.

Ope and Onnu on their wedding day

She was only a child, ten years old, when the war began and had envisioned it as something new and exciting. It soon became something very real and very frightening. She experienced the deaths of others around her and was made distinctly aware of the possibility of her own death. She saw buildings destroyed, including her own school and home. She came in contact with other cultures for the first time and found them at times to be completely pleasant and at other times to be totally evil, and so is the human race, especially during a war.

As I concluded my thoughts about Onnu's war, I thought back to the quote out of Franz Josef's diary, "What all have you lived through and what is still in front of you-you brides, wives, and mothers?" Onnu's story answered his question, but it was only one of the countless answers. There were millions of women all over Germany, all over Europe, and indeed all over the world forced to struggle to survive in a world that had been turned upside down by the war. The men they loved were sent to fight and possibly die, foreigners invaded their homes, and attaining basic necessities became a daily struggle. These were the stories of the women and children on the home front.

Georg and Onnu (2001)

Trude Hinzen von Laufenberg
February 7, 1926 - February 21, 2002

Chapter 6

Omi: A Young Woman's Suffering

One often talks of heroes among us men, bestows us with high honors and medals, but you in the homeland remain without praise hymns and outer adornments.   But there is none that would be sufficient for you.

These were the words with which Franz Josef continued his journal entry in September 1944. He declared his admiration for the women on the home front and recognized that the heroes of the war were not confined to those on the battlefields. He had not left Germany until 1943 and therefore had at least in part seen the suffering in the homeland. He had watched as many of the women were forced to support themselves and their families when their husbands or fathers were sent to fight. They were forced to be both mother and father to children who were encountering the harshest of life's realities too early in their young lives. They struggled to cook for their families when there was no food, to find shelter when their homes were destroyed, to educate their children when the schools were closed. And they waited, waiting to hear that a husband, father, brother, or friend had been killed, waiting to receive a letter from the loved one in a POW camp, waiting for the bombardments to end, waiting to hear if relatives in a nearby town had survived an air attack, waiting to see what the enemy troops would do with them, waiting for their lives to return to normal. Franz Josef believed no symbol or acknowledgement could adequately honor these women. Franz Josef's words echoed in my head as I interviewed his wife, Trude von Laufenberg (whom her grandchildren call Omi) and learned of her war story.

I had gotten to know Omi fairly well during my prior visits to Germany. She lives with her eldest son Peter and his family on a farm in the small German town of Nörvenich. Their home is only about a ten-minute drive from the Klarahof, Georg's farm, and the two families often visit one another. Omi was famous for her "Dampfnudeln" [a pastry] with plum sauce, and these delicious treats almost always accompany any visit to her home. Omi loved culture and history and often took her grandchildren to visit castles and museums. She also liked to travel and regularly went on trips. However, Omi's one outstanding trait was her overflowing happiness. She seemed to always be cheerful and greeted everyone she saw with a smile and a hug or an enthusiastic handshake. Although Germans tend to be more critical, Omi saw the positive side of everyone and every situation. It is difficult to even think about her without hearing her gentle yet wholehearted laughter.

I had already worked with Omi to type Franz Josef's diary and had already interviewed Onnu. Therefore, I was somewhat less nervous about talking to Omi about her war experiences. I was no longer afraid that she would refuse to talk about it or feel insulted by my asking. She and I went back into the computer room where we had typed the diary, and she, like Onnu, began to tell her story from the initial days of the war to the years of rebuilding afterwards without my needing to ask many questions. As I listened to Omi tell her story and of the hardships that she had faced, I gained a new understanding of and admiration for her never fading smile.

A recent photograph of Omi

Omi at her house in Nörvenich

In the Third Reich I was in an organization called the "Young Girls;" that's what the Germans called "Jungmädel." We had games and meetings together. In August 1939 we went on vacation to a German island in the North Sea. Those were some wonderful weeks. I was 13 years old then and did not yet have anything to do with politics. And then we heard the news on the radio that Poland had attacked the Germans. That gave Hitler a reason to use the German military to invade Poland. It was many, many years later before we found out that this account was made up. It was actually an organized German invasion of Poland by the Germans. It was made up. That was the beginning of the war. The campaign in Poland did not last long; it was over quickly, 18 days, but of course it just kept getting worse. I kept going to school; really everything here was normal.

Omi lived in a small town not far from where she lives now called Heppendorf with her parents, two brothers, and sister. Like all of the other grandparents, they lived on a farm. I asked her where she had been going to school when the war began.

In Bergheim. I rode my bicycle seven kilometers [a little less than 4.5 miles] *everyday, or 14 kilometers there and back with my bicycle in all kinds of weather. That wasn't easy at all. There still weren't any buses, no cars.*

When the French campaign began, 1940, we became more aware of the war because the "quartering" began. German soldiers were transferred to our towns here in Germany. That was the "quartering." There were a lot of encounters between soldiers and young girls. I was still too young, but in general. Then the first air attacks began, after the invasion of France, Belgium, and Holland, and we had a lot of restless nights. At night the sirens would go off. Then we would escape to the cellar. My brother, he was still very young, 16 or 17 years old, already had to join the anti-aircraft defense.

The boys already had to go into the service in Bergheim. Because all of our young German men were away at war, we first had the Polish come as workers, and later after the French campaign, the French also came. They were placed all over, on farms, in factories, they then did the work. We always had a good relationship with the prisoners, only that in the evenings they had to go to a camp. The sirens were actually at our house; my father was always the one who got the call. Then we had to go out onto the street and turn the siren; they were operated by hand. And that alerted the whole town; that was interesting. Can you picture how that was? Whooorrrrrwhooorrrr. Terrible.

The whole neighborhood gathered in our cellar. We were scared but also talked a whole lot. At night the signal rockets would be in the sky, and when it was bad, we heard the bombs. In '41, '42, I went south of Koblenz for my higher education, and there was nothing there to remind you of the war. We went there to learn about managing a house, cooking, gardening; that was my education. And we couldn't cook very many good things because we didn't have the ingredients anymore. We only had the opportunity to practice cooking simple things. I continued my education later on a farm near our home.

Omi later talked more about her time in Koblenz:

I went to a Landfrauenschule (an agricultural school for women) in Boppard. It is a beautiful city on the Rhine, and the vineyards that surround it are full of ruins and castles. There are a lot of hotels along the river that were all used as hospitals for the wounded soldiers. Our teacher took us to visit them, and we sang them cheerful songs. A lot of the girls went to meet with the soldiers then on the weekends. There were strawberry fields and cherry plantations in the Rhine region, but there were no workers around because of the war when it was time to harvest them in June. Therefore, they had us from the school harvest them. We were glad to do it, even though we had to begin at 5:00 in the morning and then still had to have our theoretical instruction in the afternoons. The work wasn't too hard, and we got some really good sausage, bread, and wine for doing it. So we had fun.

My mother frequently sent me a package with cakes or other goodies. Then everyone would be excited, and I shared with all of the other girls in the room. The year that I spent at the Landfrauenschule-together with 35 other girls-was very nice and full of memorable experiences.

In 1945 the war kept getting more intense, and the attacks were becoming worse. Many families lost their fathers or sons or husbands in the war. My brother was drafted when he was 17. At that time, my sister was studying in southern Germany. In the cities there wasn't much to eat anymore. Everything became scarcer, not much more to heat with. Everything became scarcer. In November 1944 Düren was completely bombed. The earth shook 20 kilometers [12.5 miles] away.

Something else unique happened that I would like to mention. It was November in 1944, and the American army was in the west and had advanced to the heights of Hürtgenwald, and there were terrible bombings and destruction. My teacher's niece-her mother was dead and her father was a soldier-had stayed behind on a farm where the front was. She had no way to get out There were soldiers all around where we were, and then when one of the troops had to go to the front, I drove with the soldiers on a truck and got the 6-year-old out and brought her to her grandparents. It was risky and dangerous because American bombers were shooting at the German troops and therefore us, too. I was just 18, and my parents didn't know that I did it.

That same month I went home. Mother had gotten sick after

she had recovered from a difficult gallbladder operation in the spring and then had relapsed. But we couldn't get a doctor to come anymore; there was no gasoline. A military doctor was stationed with us, though, and he gave her a strong dose of morphine, and Mother died because her heart stopped. Only a few family and friends could come to her burial because the bombs and grenades made it too dangerous. Then I stayed home and took care of the family, the household, and the cattle, too.

The front just kept getting closer. You didn't have any more connection to the outside world. The mail didn't run anymore; we were in a state of war. Here we had German military men everywhere. And then sometime the Americans marched in. In the meantime, a cousin of mine had already been killed in the war. One cousin was a doctor in the Balkans and had disappeared on account of terrorists. That was the last we ever heard of him. We were under constant bombardment and had to stay in the cellar. When the Americans came, we came out of the cellar with white flags, towels, to surrender.

Omi waved her hand over her head as she demonstrated how they had waved the towels in the air.

That's how we had to surrender. They brought everyone to the far end of the town and gathered us together until suddenly German grenades began exploding. There was chaos, and everyone tried to save himself and to get back home to seek shelter. Later they came and got us out of the cellar again and put part of the people in the church and the others in the school cellar. The French POW's and the Polish workers were very happy because the Americans had freed them.

Because there was no one there to help with communication, I, with my terrible English, was drug around to translate. And then they stayed there. That was terrible. At in between times we were able to look after our cows. They had to be milked. And when we came home, we found total chaos. The Americans had thrown all of the furniture out and destroyed it, and on top of the pile there was Hitler's book Mein Kampf. In the cellar the Polish, or whoever, had already stolen all of our jewelry or whatever we had; that was all gone. And I don't know how long we stayed there. After a long time, it was a good while, we were able to go home again, and then we slept on the floor. Grenades had hit at and around our house. Our dog was killed by the grenades; the prisoners managed to save themselves by taking shelter in the straw.

And it took many long, long years to complete the rebuilding. There just wasn't anything anymore, no materials. Because we were farmers, we always had something to eat. There was a lot of poverty among the population; everyone helped each other. For example, I took care of feeding two boys for a long time; they were from a family that had many children. People came from the city to the country searching for something to eat. Those who had anything tried to trade for something edible. Sometimes at night they came and took our sugar beets and potatoes out of the fields and grabbed coal and everything usable off of the freight trains. They called it "organisieren."

We didn't hear anything from my brother, nothing from my sister. You didn't know anything anymore.

Omi sat, shaking her head. I then asked her where her brothers and sister had been during the war that they had heard nothing from them.

My youngest brother was just 14 and was still at home. My sister was studying in Tübingen [southern Germany], while my other brother served somewhere in the military. Later he was between the fronts, between the Americans and the Russians, and fortunately his superiors broke up the unit and set them free to find their own way. My brother, along with another comrade fought his way through with some difficulty, staying hidden. That was at the Elbe River, where his unit was dissolved, and he fought his way back to some relatives in Erfurt, one of my mother's sisters. They took him in and hid him, though no one was allowed to hide a member of the military. Then the Russians wanted to invade Erfurt and so he had to go farther. He somehow managed to fight his way through to the West on foot. There weren't any connections. And so one day he arrived in Heppendorf on foot and completely lost.

My sister also managed to find her way home, on coal trains that had gone off course. Father was very worn-out and apathetic and depressed because of Mother's death and the complete destruction of everything and the state of war. It was just a very difficult time. We, along with people from the neighborhood, took care of our cattle. Everyone, all of the people that were still there, bound together. It was an important time of feeling like you belonged together. Everyone helped everyone else and shared everything with everyone else. A tremendous sense of community arose during this time of crisis. It was like that everywhere during the crisis. Later we always said that good has also come out of this crisis time. The people were unified and helped one another.

The American occupation meant curfews, and patrols guarded and controlled the streets. Along with that there were attempts to establish intimate relationships [with the soldiers] *although it was forbidden. The soldiers, especially the blacks, then paid them with chocolate, cigarettes, and other things.*

Omi's voice trailed off in laughter. I then asked her how long it took before everything began to be normal again.

Omi's sister-in-law who was in the BDM with a marine

For example, after the stay in the cellar with all of these people, we weren't able to take care of ourselves; it wasn't possible. Afterwards I was covered with sores that had to be operated on. Luckily I could go to my uncle in Cologne; he was a house doctor, and he then took care of me. That was all just because of the dust and dirt. So, how long did it take? I don't know. At least all of 1945. The war ended. My friend's home was actually in the east, in the eastern regions, what used to be Böhmen. She lost her home, and we took her in. She then diligently spun the wool from our sheep, and we could knit sweaters and socks. I took care of everything, the rebuilding, the kitchen, and cooking. Afterwards I organized getting the bricks to rebuild and everything. When did everything return to normal? It took a long time-until the currency devaluation on June 20, 1948. With the new D-Mark came new economic and buying power.

Omi sighed and shook her head. In my German courses, we had studied a little about the various youth organizations that had existed under the Nazi regime; I therefore decided to ask Omi if she had been in the BDM, the Bundesdeutsche Mädchen.

I was in the Bund Deutscher Jungmädel. That was for girls between 14 and 16 years old. After you turned 16, you became a member of the BDM, but I never did that because the war ended. With the Jungmädel-I led the group for our town-we sang and played games together, and in the summer you could go to exciting vacation spots. That was a lot of fun. My sister-in-law, Franz Josef's sister, had a leadership position in the BDM and was active and also involved politically.

The young men between 18 and 20 also had to do social service before going into the military. The 18 to 20 year old girls also had to work. They were brought together in a camp and were then separated to go and do different types of work-all types of social work: in hospitals and infirmaries, to farms, to families with lots of children, in factories, and so on. My sister and another sister-in-law did this.

Then, just as I had done with Onnu, I asked Omi when and how she and Franz Josef had met.

I got to know Franz Josef on January 6, 1948 at the Three Kings' Day Dance in Kerpen. He had just come back from the POW camp three weeks ago and went there with his brother and sister. My cousin had invited me to the dance. It was a fateful day-this Three Kings' Day-as it was many times in other relationships in my life. Three Kings' Day is the celebration of the arrival of the three wise men, or the three kings, at the manger in Bethlehem, and on this day, my husband-to-be met me and "arrived" in my life. He liked me, and we carried on a stimulating conversation-much to the amusement of his siblings.

Franz Josef didn't know exactly where I lived. He knew that I lived in Heppendorf, but he didn't know my last name. On the following Sunday-this is a funny story-he drove his horse and buggy along the road. He took his brother-in-law and his cousin with him for support, and he drove to Heppendorf. He knew the name Gertrud, but other than that nothing exact. They told a man passing them on the road that they were searching for a girl that had been at the farmers' dance. "Oh," this man said, "my son was also there; that could have only been Gertrud Hinzen. She lives over there." That's how he found me.

I then recalled hearing tale of another man in Omi's life and asked her, "Was there another boyfriend or guy involved?"

Yes, I had already known him for a long time. He was a college student and really liked my friend from Boppard. She was from a farm in the east, and he was studying agriculture in Bonn. She was very smart and likable, but she was a Protestant, whereas he came from a strict-believing Catholic farming family. Thus, due to the customs of that time, it was impossible for them to marry. And so it happened that he later became interested in me and tried to court me. He also got to know Franz Josef, and both cherished one another. Peter-that was his name-then asked my father for permission to marry his daughter, but I decided in favor of Franz Josef. Peter is now married and lives in Trier and is the headmaster of the agricultural school. We still visit each other, and he now says, "Yes, you belonged on a farm; that's where you were and are happy."

Perhaps there's another little story worth mentioning. After the war-maybe at the end of 1945 or 1946-as the school in my hometown was being rebuilt, they hired a teacher from the east to come and teach there. He had no belongings, no family, nothing because he was a refugee. He was given a place to live, and we took care of him. That means he ate with us until his family later came and also found lodging in the town. This teacher had a son, and we became casual friends, so that he bought me as his "Maibraut" (literally, "May bride"). That was an old tradition in which the girls were auctioned off, and the young men secured themselves of a girl to go with them to the [May Day] dance and to the parade. The girl receiving the highest bid was then the "May Queen." All of the young men planted a colorfully-decorated May tree (a birch branch) at the house of their "May brides."

So, with customs and celebrations such as this one, life in the towns began to return to normal. My youth was hard and due to the war and what came with it filled with worries and responsibilities. I could never really be young, happy, and unburdened. But then I got to know another side of life-especially with Franz Josef, Georg's grandfather. Those were the most wonderful and best years of my life from 1948 to 1955, although they were also filled with a lot of troubles and work to rebuild the home and the farm.

So Omi met Franz Josef in January of 1948; exactly one year later, on Three Kings' Day, they announced their engagement and were later married. They were married for four and a half years and had three children and one on the way when Franz Josef passed away in 1955. Omi finished the interview with the following words:

I could never really be young and happy. Mother died. I had to take care of everything. I was only 19 when Mother died. I took that very seriously. I really had to do everything afterwards; my father couldn't do anything. Then I met my husband and then seven wonderful years with him...dated for two and a half years, married for four and a half. That was my greatest time.

There was no sign of complaint or regret in her voice. She was only telling the facts as they were. She was not angry or bitter or sad but seemed grateful that she had been able to enjoy those wonderful years with Franz Josef. I thought about Omi's life. Most of the children who grew up in war-ravaged Germany had been forced to grow up quickly, but with the death of her mother, Omi had been plunged into the adult world of worry and responsibility to an even greater degree. At 19, she was forced to give up her education and begin rebuilding and managing her farm. She had to take care of her younger brother and her father and worry about what had become of her other brother and sister. With one blow, she had lost not only her mother but also her childhood. And then there was that perpetual question of why. Why did her mother have to die? Why did Omi have to give up the life that she knew? Because of the war. Her mother's condition was curable, but the war had stripped her of the possibility of receiving proper medical attention. How long did the family wonder about the whys and what ifs? Or were they too busy and too afraid, trying to stay alive themselves, to ever wonder?

Then, a few years after the tragic death of her mother, Omi married the man of her dreams. They moved to his farm in Nörvenich where she took care of the house and garden, while he worked in the fields around the home. They had three children during the first four years of their marriage, Peter, Ana, and Georg, and were expecting another. They were starting their own family; their life together was just beginning. Then, her husband, too, was taken from her, leaving her alone with the responsibility of the farm and four young children.

How had Omi survived? How had she kept going? She was so young; her life lay before her so full of promise. Within a few years, she had lost the two people dearest to her, leaving her with responsibility and worry beyond her years. I thought about Omi as I knew her. How, I thought, was she so cheerful after all that she had suffered so early in her life? I thought about the time I had spent one afternoon trying to match pairs of socks that had gotten separated in the laundry. I thought about her grin and the little shout of joy she made each time we found a match. I thought about walking with her through her garden as she pointed out each new and different flower. I thought about the smile on her face as she stared out of the kitchen window, watching her two youngest grandsons throw snowballs at one another. Maybe that was how she had kept going; maybe that was her outlook on life. She looked for the little joys amidst the daily struggles.

I then thought back to what her husband Franz Josef had written in his diary, that there was no medal or honor, no

160

hymn of praise or outer adornment that could adequately pay
tribute to what the brides, wives, and mothers in the homeland
had suffered. How much more those words would have meant
to him if he had only known what his future wife would suffer.

Omi and Franz on their wedding day

Trude Hinzen
Franz - Josef von Laufenberg

geben ihre Verlobung bekannt.

Drei Könige 1949

Hoppendorf
über Elsdorf

Närvenich
bei Düren

Franz Josef's and Omi's engagement announcement

Omi's four children a few years after Franz Josef's death;
(from left to right) Peter, Georg, Anne, Maria

In December 2001, Omi temporarily blacked out while driving her car. She went to the doctor and on December 21, 2001, three days before Christmas, she was diagnosed with a malignant brain tumor. The doctor warned her and her family that she only had months to live. Exactly two months later, on February 21, 2002, she passed away at age 76. During the weeks before her death, she told her relatives, "Franz Josef has waited long enough."

Wanda Williams Richardson
Born: August 9, 1931

Gladys Bowman Davis
Born: December 6, 1932

Chapter 7

Schoolgirls' Memories

With Onnu's and Omi's tales of the war and the image of the "homefront heroes" fresh in my mind, I came home and asked my grandmothers, Mema and Nanny, about their lives during the war. I did not expect them to have experienced the danger and turmoil that Onnu and Omi had. After all, my grandmothers were young girls thousands of miles removed from the fighting. I knew that the war had not invaded their homes, but I wondered if perhaps it had crept in and stolen an older brother or a cousin. Surely they would remember the rationing and the radio announcements. As I interviewed them, I found that their war stories were indeed short; they remembered very little. I debated about whether to even include their stories. Although the war had undeniably impacted their lives, their stories somehow seemed to be overshadowed by those of the soldiers and those on the German home front. No one had lined them up on a wall and threatened them with a machine gun; no bombs had destroyed their towns. Their lives had not been in danger. But perhaps it is for that reason that their stories are interesting, because of the stark contrast between their experiences and those of people elsewhere. And perhaps it was because they offered yet another perspective of the war: a distant war through the eyes of a child.

Mema (left) with her mother (back)
and her sister Mary (right)

Nanny (left) with
niece Barbara

I interviewed Nanny and Mema separately. They had both listened as their husbands had told their war stories. They both already knew much about their husbands' experiences and asked them questions that led them to tell me more about the war. Both of my grandmothers brought me photographs and documents relating to the war. They had taken much interest in my project, and it seemed that they had told everyone they knew about it. They had helped me in any way they could. But then, when I asked them about their war, they had surprisingly little to say.

They were both young girls when the United States entered the war, which for them is when the war began. Mema (Popo's wife) had been ten years old, and Nanny (Pa's wife) had been only nine. Both cited their young age as the reason that they remembered so little. However, Onnu had only been ten, so I knew that their young age was not the only reason. People tend to remember the big unusual events in life, those occasions that have a dramatic impact on their lives. For Onnu and Omi the war had been one of these extraordinary events; for Mema and Nanny the war had much less impact on their daily lives.

Both of their memories were often vague. Mema and Nanny only lived a few miles from one another and were both going to school during the war. Mema's parents were divorced, and she lived with her mother, two older brothers, and one older sister. According to Popo, Mema's mother owned the nightclub "up on top of the hill, and her daddy had the one down below." Nanny lived with her parents, two older sisters, and one older brother. Her father was a sharecropper, and all of the family members had to help out to make ends meet. Thus, neither of my grandmothers came from well-off or highly-esteemed backgrounds.

I decided that they would probably remember the most important events of the war best, so I began my interview with

Mema by asking her if she remembered when she had learned that Pearl Harbor had been bombed. She thought hard for a moment and then replied, pausing between the words as she searched her brain for the details:

I was ten, and I remember this big stove at Mother's nightclub, and I can just faintly remember people just bein' all upset and talkin' about the war had come and what might happen. And I was scared the Germans and all were coming here. I mean, that was my horror; I was afraid that they were going to start bombing us over here. Of course, I was just ten years old and didn't have enough knowledge really of what was going on, but I remember the Sunday that it happened very distinctly when they said that Pearl Harbor had been bombed.

I thought about Mema's response in relationship to my own young experience with a distant war, the Persian Gulf War. I, too, had been ten years old when that war had begun. I remember very clearly being angry when the television show I was watching was interrupted with the news that Iraq had invaded Kuwait. I remember fearfully counting down the days until January 15, the deadline for Iraq to pull out of Kuwait. And I remember not being able to sleep the night that the war had been declared. I crawled back downstairs to the living room where my parents were watching the news. I curled up next to my mother and told her all my fears about the war coming over here, about their bombing my house, and about people that I knew dying in the war. I had nightmares for weeks about my father being drafted and then being killed in the war. Were those the same fears and worries that Mema and Nanny had faced? I asked Nanny if she too had been afraid that the war would come here.

I guess; I don't remember enough to know. I was just a child, and I thought everything was always going to be rosy. We didn't hear all these stories, all these horror stories that you hear now and all that. We didn't even see the media; we didn't realize what was going on that much. We didn't even have a radio. And that was so far away from us.

What both Mema and Nanny remember the most about the war is their older brothers being in the military. Nanny told the story of an accident involving her brother Royce Bowman, who was known as Bow:

The thing that stands out in my mind most is Bow being in service. He's eight years older than I am. He was a pilot. He was training in a fighter jet, and he had a plane crash in Florida. Of course, they notified us that he was critically injured; the government notified us. And of course my parents could not afford a trip to Florida, and the government arranged a trip for them to go to Florida. Of course, they had probably never been out of the town hardly, and they carried them to Florida because they were expecting him not to live, but he did. And I can't remember how long it took him to recuperate from that. But that's the memories that I have of the war. And he never was sent overseas, which he would have been had he not... After that crash, he couldn't go. And he did go to Korea afterwards, and when he came back from Korea, he trained people to fly helicopters, and he retired from there as a Major. That's the biggest thing I remember of our family being in the war.

Mema's brothers, James Bair and T.V., had also been in the military during the war.

James Bair, he went in the navy about the time he graduated from high school in '45. He joined the Navy in '45, but the war was probably over by the time he joined, but they were still drafting people, so he joined the Navy rather than be drafted.

I interrupted, "So when you were drafted, you had no choice what you went into?" Popo answered from his own experience, "They put you where they need you most; most of the time it was the infantry." Mema continued:

But if you joined before they drafted you, then you had a choice. James Bair was discharged after ten months because of some kind of leg injury he had or something. He got an honorable discharge, a medical discharge. And then he came back and went to school at Martin [the University of Tennessee at Martin, a 45 minute drive from Gadsden] on the GI bill. If you had served in the military, you could take advantage of the GI Bill of Rights. He went to Martin for two years, and back then it was a junior college. Then he went to [the University of Tennessee at] Knoxville.

Mema then began telling the story of her other brother T.V.

T.V. was in the war, and he joined the Navy to keep from being drafted, and he was in the Pacific on a destroyer. He was on a PT Boat, and I don't know how long T.V. was overseas. Was his boat torpedoed? I don't know much about his war story. But I know Marian, his wife, lived with me and Mother and my sister Mary.

(Both pictures above) Mema as a young girl

Nanny with her future sister-in-law Genrose Davis Boyd

Today Uncle T.V. and Aunt Marian live in Gadsden and attend the same church as the rest of my family and I do. As Mema talked about what she knew about his being in the war, I thought about one Sunday around Veterans' Day in which the pastor had asked all of the veterans to come to the front. He asked them to take turns telling when and how they had served their country. When it was Uncle T.V.'s turn, he began to cry. Popo was the only other man to do the same. Had the war experiences of Mema's brother been as bad as Popo's, so that he could not talk about them? Had he also lived through many years of silence? Was it for that reason that Mema knew so little about what he had done in the war?

The other major part of the war that the two of them remembered was the rationing and the scarcity of certain goods. I asked Nanny if her family had been affected by the rationing since they were farmers. She answered by telling me of a particular situation that she remembered.

I can remember my grandfather, he was on the old-age pension, that's what they called it then. It was some type of relief, and he would come to visit us. Of course, we raised most of our meat, kept 'em in the smokehouse, and my grandfather would come, and we would walk through the fields. I wasn't even big enough then hardly to work. There was a little store down by our house, and he'd go get me bologna, and I thought that was a big, big treat. We had country ham and all that but no bologna.

Mema told me of her experience with rationing:

We had ration books that you had to buy gas and shoes and groceries. You could get so many canned goods with your ration stamps, and so much gas. And what else was rationed? Tires. And you could buy stuff on the black market; there were some people who did that. And I remember there used to be a big old gas tank, gas trucks that used to deliver gas from Memphis to Camden, and they used to stop up at the dance hall, and there'd still be some gas in them after they delivered the tanks. They'd park it where it'd drain, and we could drain gas out in big ol' buckets. I remember sellin' some to Edward Williams, and we'd sell that gas because they'd give it to us. Those truck drivers would stop and let us drain what was left out of there.

In order to follow up my question about what they remembered about the war's beginning, I decided to ask my grandmothers if they remembered when the war had ended. Mema answered:

See, I was just 14 when the war was over, and I remember the day the war was over. There used to be buses that went by our house to the Milan Arsenal, where I worked for 34 years [after the war was over]. At that time they had buses running from Brownsville to Milan, picking up people along the highway that worked at the arsenal, makin' bullets. They called it the "Bullet Plant," and I can remember people catching the buses all up and down the highway. I remember I was standing in the front yard when I heard it. It seems like there was this bus that came from Milan, and there was a lady, Elsie Brown, that got off in front of our house. They were all shoutin' and hollerin', and that's where I learned that the war had ended, those people that were comin' in, those that was makin' the ammunition. Or maybe I had heard it, and I was the one who told them on the bus. There was something about being out in the yard when that bus stopped.

When she had finished, Popo added, "A lot of people didn't want the war to end because that was the only decent job they'd ever had, and they didn't want to lose that job."

When I asked Nanny about the end of the war, she too was uncertain of the details.

I remember coming home from school and of course, communication was far from what it is now, but we knew that the war was over. I can remember that; it was a real happy time, but I don't know the exact details.

I ended the interviews, as I had with Onnu and Omi, by asking my grandmothers how they had met their husbands. They both seemed to remember every detail from the first date to the time they married. Because my grandfathers were with them during the interview, there were several discussions that I found somewhat amusing about the finer points, the exact whens and wheres and with whoms.

Mema began her story:

When the war broke out in '41, I was just ten years old. I knew who Porter was, but of course, I didn't have much to do with him. Porter came back home from the army in '46, and I wasn't but fifteen then, and I was going with another guy, but Porter said, "Some time I would like to have a date with you, if you're not goin' with him," or something. So we had our first date on Easter, 1947. So see, he'd been back from the army for a year before I ever dated him. We went to Bells to the movie, and then we dated for two years from '47 to '49, and we got married June 3. And I had his girlfriend's that he had when he was in the war, I had her watch, and I still have it in there, and of course, I don't know who all he went with before he went with me after he got back from the service. So his war experience was all over with before I ever knew him because I was just a kid.

Porter and I went to Erin, Tennessee, and Brother Carl married us in June. And I wasn't 18, I was just 17, and my birthday wasn't 'til August, but Brother Carl had said that he could get our marriage license. My sister Mary and her husband Charles lived in Clarksville at the time. Erin was not too far from Clarksville, so we went to Mary and Charles' on June 3, that morning. So we went to Erin about 6:30, and we went to the house and were told, "They're down at the courthouse waitin' for ya'll; they wouldn't let him have them." So we drove down there, and he was sittin' out under the tree on a Coca-Cola case waiting for us to come. The lady who issued the marriage licenses was still in the courthouse waiting on us. We got married in Erin and then went on our honeymoon to Knoxville.

That's what when we go to these veterans' reunions, a lot of people will say, "Were y'all married when he was in service?" And I'll say "Naw. I was just 13 when he went off." I knew Porter's brother Ponvelle a whole lot better than I knew Porter. Porter was seven years older than I am, and Ponvelle only four. Of course, you know, the girls usually get older boys.

Nanny had also found one of those "older boys." When I asked her to tell the story of how she had met Pa, Pa began to say something. Nanny quickly interrupted, "Don't tell that," and I laughed trying to imagine what could have happened that she did not want him to tell me. She began the story:

We met on a blind date. Larry Todd [a friend] had a date with a girl, and he didn't have a car and couldn't go. He told Jim if he would carry him, he would get him a date. And he got him a date with me. And I worked at the dime store that night. It was on a

*Saturday night, and when I got off at the dime store, they was sittin'
out front, and Larry came got me. Jim was down there where a car
had had a wreck, and I was in his car when they come back.*

Pa interrupted, "Well see, you told me not to tell that."
Nanny replied, "Well, I wanted to tell it my way." Nanny
continued:

*We met after he'd been drafted. He'd already gone back to school
that year. He'd already gone back to school and graduated. Seems to
me like he worked at Shelton's [a local store]'bout the time we met
and got married because he bought our furniture through Shelton's.
He went to Memphis and bought our furniture through a wholesale
house before we married, all except our refrigerator. We had our
furniture paid for, but we bought our refrigerator on credit. That's
about all he's ever bought on credit. He decided we wasn't ever
gonna get that paid for.*

I laughed, thinking about what I knew about my
grandfather's spending habits. He had paid for his house and
every car that he had ever bought up front with cash, and he
does not own a credit card. Pa broke in to add, "I forget how
much I had saved up when we got married. See, I farmed
about ten or twelve acres of cotton and worked at Shelton's,
too." Nanny explained, "We didn't spend a lot of money when
we was datin'." With a look of unbelief, Pa exclaimed, "Spent
three dollars most of the time." My grandmother good-
humoredly rolled her eyes and continued:

*Ya'll bought that Oldsmobile before we married, because you came out to
show me that new car. He came out to show me his new car one night, and
we was gonna ride up the road and had a flat tire. Brand new car.*

Nanny and Pa (couple in the middle) together with
friends Larry and Barbara Todd

Mema and Popo (left and middle)
during their dating years

Pa broke in, "Them old bridges out there where she lived had them old nails on 'em. You crossed one, runnin' 30 miles an hour, and it sounded like you was runnin' 80. Of course, I was always late." Nanny added, "They gave him a bad name out there in that Bethel community, 'Speed Demon' There wasn't too many cars out there." Pa, needing to justify himself, said, "I never did drive fast. Well, everyone of 'em [the bridges] was loose and would just rattle like everything."

After hearing their stories about dating, I asked them how long they had dated before they were married. "About ten years," my grandfather answered quickly. Nanny shot him a curious look and corrected his exaggeration, "Uh, 2 years. I was 17 years old." "Did you quit school?" I asked. "Yeah, but that year I quit school, I had to help finish the crop out. My daddy went to work as a carpenter, and I had to quit and help finish the crop out." Pa and Nanny were married in Erin, Tennessee, in December 1949, only a few months after Popo and Mema had also been married there.

As I ended the interviews, I began questioning the significance of my grandmothers' war experiences. As I talked to others who had also been children on the American home front, I found that my grandmothers' memories were fairly typical. Most of them had one or two encounters that they remembered vividly, but most of their memories of life during the war had faded with time. Neither of my grandmothers had had a particularly easy childhood. Mema had not had an ideal family situation, and Nanny's family had been extremely poor. But even as they expressed the difficulties of this era in their lives, there was a sense of nostalgia in their voices as they talked about the simplicity of life back then, of not having to lock their doors, of not owning a car, and of buying two pieces of bubble gum for a penny. The feelings they expresse reminded me very much of the manner in which Omi had

Memaw and Popo's
wedding picture

Pa and Nanny on their wedding day

talked about the sense of community that had prevailed during those difficult years.

After she married, Nanny had two children (my mother and her younger brother Mike). When her children were still young, she became a licensed practitioner nurse (LPN) and began working for $32 a week. She remained a nurse all of her life until she retired in 1995. However, she still works part-time as a nurse and devotes much of her time to visiting and taking care of the sick from her church and in her community. Her four grandchildren think about how important it is to her to be there for all of the meaningful events of their lives, every basketball or baseball game, every band concert, every graduation or awards' ceremony. They remember all of the times that she worried about the dinners on Christmas Eve, Thanksgiving, and Easter, although they always turned out wonderful. I think about the times we have spent with her and Pa at their cabin on the Tennessee River and the days she stayed with us when we were sick and had to stay home from school. Today Nanny is active in her small local church, where she oversees the nursery and is on various committees. She is always looking to help those who need her help.

Mema married and then began working at the arsenal in Milan, Tennessee. She had three children, Gary, Jan, and Bruce (my father). After she retired from the arsenal, she found it impossible to stay home and started working for the local grocery store. She worked there until 1998 when her great-granddaughter Page was born. She now happily takes care of Page several days a week and always speaks with enthusiasm about Page's latest accomplishments. Mema is outgoing and friendly; she talks to everyone who sits down beside her and seems to be able to find out a person's life history in a few short minutes. She, like Nanny, has always attended all of her grandchildren's activities. She too is actively involved in the church as the church treasurer. Her grandchildren remember fondly all of the Christmas breakfasts and Thanksgiving dinners at her house, the homemade strawberry jam, and the banana pudding.

In recent years Mema has also become an active participant in Popo's veterans' organizations. She often sends information to those wanting to know about Popo's combat unit, people whose fathers, brothers, and other relatives had served with him. As I put this project together, she become enthusiastically involved and searched for whatever materials she thought I could use. She encouraged Popo to talk about his war story and bridged the silence when he broke down and could not continue. I began to ask myself why. Why was she so interested in helping me with this undertaking? Why was she so involved in the veterans' organizations? It was not her story, or was it? Could it be that she too was searching for answers? She had lived with this man for fifty years, hearing very little about his years of combat. These years had obviously had a huge impact on his life and had shaped the very person that he was, but until recent years she knew almost nothing about his war stories. She had reared three children with him, had woken up with him every morning, and eaten dinner with him every night, yet there was always this silence. Mema had experienced very little of the war; she hardly even remembered it. However, she wants to more. Naturally she was interested in all of it on Popo's behalf, but perhaps she is also searching for answers for herself, answers to the questions that she hasn't been able to ask for more than fifty years.

Recent picture of Nanny and Pa
with their two grown chidren Mike and Reta

Recent pictures of Mema and Popo with their youngest
grandson Chad on his graduation day

The Author (bottom row, center) with her family

Conclusion

When I began the original research for this project in the fall of 1999 (before I had interviewed my grandfather), I visited a bookstore. I wanted to learn what information was available concerning the common soldiers of World War II. What types of memoirs, testimonials, and research books had already been written? I had been planning to head immediately for the military history section of the bookstore, but when I walked in, I was confronted with a display advertising the current best-selling book. I was drawn to the display because of the black-and-white photograph on the front cover of a smiling soldier reading a letter. His helmet was lying beside him containing the picture of a woman (obviously his wife or girlfriend). It was Tom Brokaw's book The Greatest Generation Speaks (the sequel to his first best-selling book The Greatest Generation). As I thumbed through it, I found that it was a book of personal stories of Americans who had been involved in many different aspects of the war. The book told their stories through letters they had written to Mr. Brokaw in response to the original book.

The best-selling book in the United States at that time was a collection of short personal World War II stories, mostly the stories of common people. What did that signify concerning Americans' interest in the war? They obviously wanted to know, but who wanted to know and why? I received an answer to my question the next time I went home from college. On a visit to Mema and Popo's house, I saw Tom Brokaw's book lying open on the table beside Popo's recliner. My uncle had given it to him as a present. After Popo had finished it, he gave it back to my uncle because he wanted to read it. My uncle then gave it to me, and I passed it on to my father. I am not sure who has it now, but it is probably still circulating among members of my family. Why? Why did three different generations want to read that book, a book of memories? Each generation was searching for different answers in those little stories. Popo later told me that neither that book nor any of the other war books (such as those by Steven Ambrose) he had read ever mentioned his unit. Perhaps he was searching for a story like his, someone with whom he could identify. Maybe the books were for him a type of group therapy, a way to see that others had had similar experiences and had suffered similar consequences. My father and uncle were both interested in World War II history and were searching to know and understand their father. Despite always having had a very good relationship with Popo, there was a part of him that they did not know, that they could not know. They hoped to receive a glimpse of this missing piece by reading the stories of those who had witnessed similar circumstances. And what was it that I wanted to know? I, like the generation before me, wanted to understand my grandfather better. I wanted to know why he did not and could not talk about it. But more deeply I wanted to know how my life was a reflection of Popo's and of my other grandparents. What had they been that caused me to be what I am? How did their world impact mine?

My family was obviously not the only family interested in these stories of the war, and Tom Brokaw's books were not the only ones recently published about the war. As Americans see the World War II veterans dying daily before their eyes, there has emerged an obsession in the American media with the personal stories of this generation. They no longer want these men and women portrayed as the glorious, exalted heroes, as they were when they returned home. Rather, as obvious from recent movies, such as Steven Spielberg's Saving Private Ryan (1998) and Terrence Malick's The Thin Red Line (1998), Americans are seeking to learn about the real side of the war, all of the violent, gruesome, and mundane realities. They are looking for the experiences of the common soldiers, as seen in the popularity of Stephen Ambrose's Citizen Soldiers describing the events of the war based on interviews with the enlisted soldiers who were there. Many recently-published memoirs of the war have also been widely read, such as Tracy Sugarman's My War, in which the author uses the letters and sketches he sent to his wife during the war to tell his love story and his war story.

Although the war literature in America has become more realistic and less glorified during recent decades, most of the authors still use an approach such as the one used by Tom Brokaw, referring to these soldiers and home front survivors as the "Greatest Generation." As I thought about this term in correlation with my own research, I began to wonder-if the American World War II generation was the "Greatest Generation," what did that make the same generation in Germany-the worst?

The war literature in Germany obviously differs tremendously from that in the United States. They cannot praise any heroes but rather can only search for the more and less guilty. Few of the veterans on the battlefield or on the home front want to discuss their activities in the war, and if they do desire to tell their stories, they must ask themselves if their children want to hear about them. The war left Germany devastated, not only politically and economically, but also emotionally. The German people had not only lost their men in the battles; they had also lost their sense of identity. In Germany, there is not a sense of trying to hide the war or to cover up the guilt (at least not publicly); the facts and consequences of the war are presented openly and frequently.

There is a whole literary movement in Germany that deals with the problems and consequences of the war. This movement is referred to as Vergangeheitsbewältigung, or the process of dealing with one's past and includes the process of acknowledging, portraying, and overcoming the past. Wolfgang Borchert's Draußen vor der Tür analyzes the problems that German soldiers faced when they returned home. Authors such as Christa Wolf and Siegfried Lenz, both children of the generation that was actively involved in the war, use fictional works to portray the real problematic German national identity and their search to discover who they are and how they fit into the postwar society.

However, there is something missing from the German bookshelves-the personal stories of the soldiers and home front survivors. There are few German books, such as those by Tom Brokaw and Stephen Ambrose, that relay the stories of the common soldiers. When Germans talk about the war, they discuss its overriding political principles, rarely mentioning their individual encounters. I was able to find one book in the museum shop of the Haus der Geschichte der Bundesrepublik Deutschland (the History Museum of the Federal Republic of Germany), entitled Krieg: Erzählungen aus dem Schweigen (War: Tales out of the Silence) by Carl Schüddekopf that contains interviews with fourteen common German soldiers. I am sure there are other such books, but they do not become bestsellers, as do their American counterparts. There are a few well-known memoirs of German soldiers, such as those by Guy Sajer (The Forgotten Soldier) and Siegfried Knappe

(Soldat), but even these are more widely read in the United States than in Germany.

If Popo turns to the war books, to the experiences of others, to find himself and to deal with the emotional scars of the war, where did Georg's grandfathers turn? Neither Franz Josef nor Ope suffered the gruesome combat that Popo had, but many German soldiers had. What did they read? With whom did they talk? My parents' generation searches for the stories of their parents in the literature and in the media. However, few of Georg's parents' generation are searching for their parents' stories. Perhaps they rebelled against those war experiences or perhaps they chose to ignore them, but few have tried to find out about them. After all, who wants to or is able to accept their parents as having any part, however small, in all of the evils of the Nazi party? And Georg, how does he respond? He has shown some interest. He was present for most of the interviews and asked questions. Through the months, he has read all of our grandparents' stories. But it was not something he would have ever done on his own; he would have never asked his grandmothers.

As I attempt to conclude this long emotional journey, I cannot help reflecting on all that I have learned along the way. I have come to a new understanding of the Second World War and of those who participated in it. I can no longer think of this war or of these people in the obscure, clichéd terms that traditional movies and history books have used to describe them, for they talk of honor and courage, heroes and patriotic duty. It is not that the soldiers and the home front survivors were not honorable and courageous. Many were heroes, and many served and sacrificed out of a sense of patriotic duty.

However, all of those terms faded to nothing more than a superficial din in the presence of Popo's tears. They sounded so hollow next to Franz Josef's and Ope's expressions of longing and grief. Those words described a war that had existed in the newspapers and in the political offices, not the war that our grandparents had fought and survived. The war that Georg's and my grandparents described was not a war of national pride or heroism, but rather a war of laughter and tears, mostly tears. It was a war of killing, of dying, of guilt, of sadness, of uncertainty, and of loneliness.

During my research I was repeatedly confronted with the fact that our grandparents had not been the stern-faced men and women that I had so often seen in World War II movies. They had been boys and girls. With each grandparent that I interviewed, I heard over and over again, "I was 19 when I was drafted," "I was 19 when my mother died and I was left in charge of the farm," or "I was 14 when the Americans invaded our home." Even after hearing their stories, I had still envisioned them as adult men and women. It took a long time before the revelation struck me that I had been 19 when I had begun my research. It seemed impossible that they could have been my age (or younger) during the tragic experiences that they had described. Popo and Ope had only been Georg's age when they had been drafted, but Georg seemed much too young to be in such a war.

This journey also brought me face-to-face with the stories and the families of the German soldiers, the soldiers who are always killed without thought or feeling in the war movies and books. Through Franz Josef's diary and Ope's letters, I met two of the men who had made up the monstrous Nazi army, the men almost always portrayed as cold-blooded, ruthless killers without families or feelings. I was allowed to see the war from their perspective, through their eyes. They were young men just like Popo, forced to leave their families and homes and ordered to fight. They had suffered many of the same fears and tragedies that my grandfather had. The German soldiers committed many atrocities during the war, but as Popo had said, "We [the Americans] were taught to be mean, just like Georg's granddaddies were taught." With each enemy soldier I see killed in the final triumphant scene of a war movie, I cannot help but thinking of the faces and the stories of Georg's grandfathers.

I thought back to Popo's original inquiry that had led to my years of research, "Did your grandfather steal my Christmas package?" I knew that it was not possible for Georg's grandfathers to have been among those German soldiers that had stolen those presents, but was it possible that our grandfathers' paths had ever crossed? Maybe just for a moment, possibly at a port while boarding or disembarking from ships, or while Franz Josef traveled through the United States by train, maybe they had somewhere along the way met; maybe their eyes had crossed for only a moment. Would they have believed what the future would hold, that their grandchildren would some day be married? Some day Georg and I hope to have children. When they learn about World War II in school, what will we tell them about their great-grandparents?

As I end this project and this journey through the past and the present, I know that the memories will never leave me. I will always remember the tears on Popo's cheeks, his overwhelming expression of horror and grief. I will never forget the longing, the sadness, and the wisdom of Franz Josef's diary or the simpler expressions of the same feelings found in Ope's letters. I will always remember the oblivious expression on Pa's face as he shook his head to each of my questions about the war. The memories of the voices, the faces, and the gestures of Onnu and Omi during my interviews with them will also always remain with me-how their faces wrinkled with fear as they talked about the bombings, how Onnu ducked her head in her arms as she explained how they had lain in the bomb craters, and how Omi pretended to wave her white flag in the air and demonstrated the noise of the sirens. I will remember Nanny and Mema's thoughtful faces as they sought desperately to piece together the elements that had made up their childhoods. I will always carry all of their stories with me; they have become a part of me. I will never know all of the names, the dates, or the battles of the Second World War, but I will never forget the eternal expressions of the war, the expressions of our grandparents-their faces, their emotions, their handwritten thoughts-all seeking to explain the tears and the silence.

Betsy Richardson Pingen was born in Jackson, Tennessee in 1980. She spent all of her childhood and teenage years in the West Tennessee area, never more than a few minutes drive from all of her grandparents, aunts, uncles and cousins. Inspired by her family's love for sports and the outdoors, she spent most of her youth either playing on all types of athletic teams or just trying to outswim and outfish her brother, Chad, only thirteen months her junior. Besides sports, Betsy's other passion was learning other languages, which exhibited itself early when she began teaching herself sign language at age 7. This passion continued to grow until she had the opportunity to take Spanish her ninth grade year at Jackson Christian School, a small high school that at the time had only 200 students. However, her language interest quickly turned to German when she began dating a German exchange student, Georg, her senior year.

After graduating from high school in 1998, Betsy and Georg attended college together at Samford University in Birmingham, Alabama, where the two stayed three years. They continued dating and were engaged in November of 2000. During this time Betsy began seriously studying German and developed the language abilities necessary to complete the research for this book. She graduated in 2001 with a B.A. in

German with the highest honors in her class, while Georg completed the first part of a Dual Degree Engineering Program between Samford and Washington University.

In August of 2001, the couple moved to St. Louis, Missouri, where they attended Washington University. Betsy completed a one-year program for her Masters of Arts in Teaching degree, while Georg finished his B.S. in Mechanical Engineering. The two married on June 29, 2002 in Gadsden, Tennessee, in the church Betsy had attended with her family since infancy. They were surrounded by friends and family, including Georg's parents, four siblings, aunt, uncle, and best friend who were all able to fly in from Germany. The couple is still living in St. Louis. Betsy is now teaching German and Spanish at Clayton High School, and Georg is completing his Masters in Mechanical Engineering.